A Prodigal Princess

My Journey to Finding Purpose and Peace

Adara L. Butler

To my Dad and my Mom:

For letting me fly free to find my wings and find my way.

You trained up your child in the way she was supposed to go.

Even though she lost her way for a little bit she never forgot it.

Thank you for loving me, your prodigal princess, unconditionally.

With all of my love always,

Adara

ℰ☯ℭℬ
ℳac Ꮶenzie Ꝑublishing

Acknowledgements

First and utmost, off of the top I have to give Honor to God the head of my life and give honor and praise to my Savior Jesus Christ for saving, delivering and setting me free.

I have to give honor to my Pastors who I have the double blessing of being their daughter; Pastors Darren Ellis and Patricia K Butler. Dad and Mom, I love you so very much and words can never express how thankful I am for you. I pray this book touches millions of people's hearts but that it first touches yours and you know all the sacrifices you made were not in vain. Everything you instilled in me was not lost. I am where I am, and I am who I am today because of your love.

To Qiana, Kimberly, DJ; my siblings; I love you all and no matter how many friends I make in life you are still my first friends and my first ministry. Forever and always will I cherish the way we grew up together, the way we used to plot to get each other in trouble and our hilarious impersonations of 'The Parents' behind their backs.

To my nephews and nieces Isaiah, Jordan, Kennedi, Janise; Aunty loves you SO very much and although I don't have children you all keep me young and well equipped should that day come.

To my grandmothers Bernice and Mary C thank you for all your prayers and love.

To my grandmothers in love "Nana" and "Mama Willa" both of you have been so instrumental in my life and I thank you for all your prayers and love.

To my Godparents: Arthur and Ann-Marie Butler and Bernice (Candy) Butler thanks for everything you do. Thank you for stepping in and being great second parents. I blame you all for the embarrassing family photos of me but I do forgive you.

To my entire extended family (all four thousand of you if both sides were combined); to ALL OF YOU I love you and thank you for supporting me. I can't list all of ya'll so charge it to my page count and not my heart.

To my very best friend in the whole entire world, Imani Z. Anglin words cannot truly capture the essence of what you are to me or why I love you so much. Thank you for being a friend and teaching me how to be a friend. A huge part of the reason I am the way I am today is because of you. Thank you for walking with me throughout life. Forever and always you'll be the peanut butter to my jelly. I still believe God will make a way for us to live down the block from each other again at some point just like we did growing up. "Vatos Locos Forever."

To John J. Momplaisir: Thank you for being you. No long dramatic speech is needed here; you already know (you don't like to read long anyways). But thank you for being you. YOU are appreciated and have impacted my life in more ways than you know.

To my twin sister in the spirit Kristy T. Butler; you came into my life at a time I needed you the most. Stepping into this new dimension, I was praying for a sister in ministry who understood me, my mission, my ministry, and my life who would push me and I could do the same for her. I tell you often in private but I celebrate your life here publicly. I am so excited for what is coming for YOU. I thank God for your friendship and the divine connection we have. I love you Kris and no matter what the family tree says somehow, someway we are related in real life girlfriend!

To two incredible writers who inspired and pushed me to push through; Curtrice Williams and Richard Taylor Jr., thank you for being instrumental in my process of finally sitting down to put the work and effort in to finish this book and do what I was supposed to do. Watching you handle your business and write your books blessed me more than you will ever know. You both are an inspiration and blessing to many including little 'ole me.

To Catherine MacKenzie and Patricia M. Woodside; thank you for working so hard with me and for me on this project. I know I asked a lot of questions, sent many emails and texts, and wanted a lot done in a short period of time but you both were so gracious and diligent through this whole process. Thank you for treating my vision like it was your own. I thank God for you both being in the delivery room and helping me safely (and in my right mind) deliver my book baby.

Finally, I dare not forget to acknowledge anyone else not mentioned who has supported me in any way. To each and every person who believes in me and supports me in any way, shape, or form; from the bottom of my heart I say I love you and thank you.

Yours Truly,

Adara Butler

Table of Contents

Foreword

Life within a family is designed to be a very pleasant experience. However, there are times when it is not so pleasant. One of those instances can be when a child is prodigal. It is an "unwanted reality" for both the parent and the child. When it happens, it is very difficult for all concerned. One of the most pressing difficulties for everyone involved is the answer to the question: "how do I handle this?". The intensity of the question pulsates from day to day as everyone is living in the "unwanted reality" because of the unpredictability of the "prodigal's" actions.

I remember vividly the days when our daughter Adara went through the stage of being "prodigal". As parents, especially Christian parents, we never would have imagined that this stage would ever occur in her life. Nevertheless, it happened, becoming unquestionably an "unwanted reality" for us. It was not what we had dreamed of her, it was nightmarish, and often we could not envision a solution of managing it ourselves as well as getting her out of it as quickly as possible. We often navigated days of pain, hurt, embarrassment, anger, bewilderment, shame, disappointment and a myriad of other rollercoaster emotions and attitudes. I often asked myself, "where did I fail her as her father?" There were many "hand-wringing" nights because of nervous speculation of "what is she into now?" There were days I wanted to scream "snap out of it!" but I could not for fear of it becoming fuel for the fire to drive the wedge between us deeper. I had to learn how to accept the futility of too much direct tangible intervention, and rest in the knowledge of the effective intangibility of prayer. For a father, this is really challenging because your instincts are to jump right in feet first, getting directly involved until the situation is fixed according to your satisfaction. I remember often wondering how long it was going to be like this. Even though my faith dictated adopting an outlook of patient optimism, my feelings at times ignited a fear of hopeless cynicism. It was an intense internal battle navigating the days of this "unwanted reality." I tried at times (often unsuccessfully) to imagine what this stage was like for her, in the hopes of finding and bringing a resolution to this phase from a different angle. Additionally, that approach brought even more frustration because Adara was at times unable to articulate what she was going through herself.

BUT, THINGS CHANGED. And just like that, as long as it seemed to last, that much quicker, the "unwanted reality" was over. Just like the Biblical "prodigal", Adara *came to herself!* Looking back on those days now, I can honestly say that things weren't as bad as I thought. Because of the benefit of hindsight, I see the experience in a totally different light. I have so much peace with that stage of her experience. I have inwardly reconciled myself to the reality that it had to be. Mainly, I realize it was a very necessary ingredient for Adara's growth and development and a critically essential piece to the foundation of her life's assignments. As bizarre as this may sound, without her prodigal experience, I do not believe Adara would be as effective in fulfilling her purpose had she not gone through what she went through. And at the risk of sounding self-serving and biased because she is my daughter, she has become (and is becoming) a phenomenal young woman who is clearly on a greatly-positive and realistic mission. Her acceptance of and commitment to that mission could have very well been aborted had she not went through the life-stage of being "prodigal". If only I had known then, what I know now; if only there had been something documented to help me navigate that season of "unwanted reality"; if only there had been something documented that could relevantly speak to her as the "prodigal"...

Adara, has written this wonderful book, that addresses the "if only's" that I couched previously. She has written this book to help the parent, child, and everyone concerned navigate this challenging and at times very painful part of family life that happens to many of us. She is very candid, blunt, and transparent about her experiences of being a "prodigal" and the "unwanted realities" it created for her and subsequently us, her parents and family.

I am extremely honored and proud of Adara. I am honored, proud, delighted and elated as her father, to present this book to every, parent, child or person who is presently living in the experience of "unwanted realities" because of the "prodigal" experience. When her mother and I navigated this season in her life, we had to realistically revisit our dreams of her, reject the nightmares of those prodigal experiences with her and repeatedly rehearse a vision of a new day for her. We had to do this with unconditional love, patience and prayer, resting in the promise of Scripture to train up a child, Provs. 22:6. Interestingly that verse of Scripture promises the child will not depart; it never promises that the child will not detour. Therein lies the vision.

Adara is going to take you on a wonderfully intriguing but realistic journey that will give you that vision into the transforming finality that God has destined for her, AND YOUR PRODIGAL SITUATION. Prayerfully, as you read this book, you will find a vision of hope and peace for your "unwanted reality" with your "prodigal" situation, believing that whatever place you occupy in this situation, that it will not always be like this! Settle in and walk with her through these pages of <u>A Prodigal Princess: My Journey To Finding Purpose and Peace.</u>

Pastor Darren E Butler, Sr.
"Pastor Daddy"

Introduction

This is not a book intended to beat you over the head with Scripture or preach doom and destruction if you don't conform to a particular doctrine or denomination within the Body of Christ. There are plenty of books out there like that. I'm sorry to disappoint anyone who's looking for a book that's going to give you fifty million do's and don'ts for being a godly man or woman or even "a good person."

This is not that book.

Nor will any of the other books I hope to publish be that way, but I can say definitely not this one.

I am still figuring out what it means to walk this walk called "being a Believer," and this book is a collection—a devotional journal with prayers, if you will—of the pieces of my Believer's walk I've gotten past and can now share. I definitely don't have this walk all figured out. Nobody does...and don't let anyone make you believe they do. Being a Christian, loving God and living a life of purpose and peace is a daily exercise. It's an exercise of faith and love. It's a choice you make every day in your mind and heart. It's no different than choosing to get up every day and go to work or school. We do those things because we have to. When we recognize our need for God, pursuing Him and living for Him become things we *have* to do. Something we choose to do...indefinitely.

My book is a very candid, open and transparent story about my life and how I, a preacher's daughter, born and raised in the church, went from rock bottom and feeling lost to a place of contentment and satisfaction. Some of the pieces of my testimony are found in various posts on my Instagram and Facebook pages, but this book will be all of it. This is the raw, hard, cold truth about me and how I hit the ground, but got back up. My hope and prayer is you will be encouraged and feel empowered after reading this.

I wrote this book to minister to and encourage others and to let you know you are not alone in the everyday struggles you face. I especially have a soft spot for preacher's children because, on top of all the pressure we face from society just as people, there's so much pressure from church people for preacher's children. Church people are just something extra special sometimes. Although the softest spot in my heart is for my fellow "preacher's kids," I wrote this to prayerfully and hopefully encourage and minister to all types of people. All of us, in some way, shape or form, are prodigal until we find our way back to God through salvation through Jesus Christ.

Now, if you are squeamish...don't read this. I refuse to be responsible for you falling out and fainting, so if you get lightheaded by what you read, go ahead and drop this book right now. There will be some parts of this book that get really dirty and ugly. It's going to shock you—and that's okay. The good news is I am well past those dirty, uncomfortable, difficult parts that it took me a long time to even share. Even better news is that if you are a person who struggles with or can relate to any of this, there is hope and there're solutions to our problems. If you are a super saint who's been saved and sanctified and filled all your life and came into the world wearing an all-white long skirt to the ground, then please don't read this book because this is not for you.

So if you are a person who's struggled...

- With self-esteem and self-worth
- With knowing right from wrong...and blatantly choosing wrong
- With substance addictions and alcohol
- With looking for love in relationships, in sex and 'situation-ships'
- With wondering why you were even born

- With wondering if you are loved or capable of loving others
- With wondering if God is really real and if He really cares about you
- With wanting to serve and love God, but still have your 'fun'
- With finally choosing God over everything, but still falling short and messing up
- With being a Christian and dealing with traumatic experiences that rock your world and shake your faith

If any of these are your current struggles, I have got just the book for you. I promise it's a good read and not just because I wrote it. (Well, okay, that's part of the reason it's good, but not the only reason.) It's a good read because I give you real, hardcore, blunt truth.

I've always been a very blunt person, even as a child. I've been through all the things listed above so I can relate, and in this book, I will tell you what helped me get through.

I know you're thinking, "Okay...How could she have been through all of that, *all* of those things above?"

I can and I was. *All* of them. Yes, honey, the little preacher lady/pastor's daughter—me, Miss Encourager—I've been through some things. Go figure. But I have to let you in on a secret: preacher's kids and pastor's kids are people too. We struggle. We cry. We make mistakes. We need love and grace as much as the next person.

This "good girl" with the baby face and chubby cheeks who people say has no traces of the old life she used to live, was a bad girl for a few years. I didn't always look like this...literally. I'm so glad we don't have to look like what we've been through because if we did, I would look so ugly. Butt ugly. I would smell ugly (which I don't in real life. I believe in the ministry of soap and water three times daily.) If we actually looked and smelled like our pasts, I would reek of pain and hurt. I don't because I got free from all of the hurt and painful things that happened to me.

So with that said, go ahead, get comfortable and turn the page. You'll laugh because I'm a jokester, but you might cry too and that's okay. I cried a lot during those painful years. The awesome news is I'm not crying so much anymore. I hope my story, my "prodigal princess" journey, is encouraging and touches you wherever you are in your journey.

Love, *Adara*

Chapter 1

Identity Crisis

Not knowing who you are can be scary. For a long time, I didn't know who I really was. I mean, of course I knew my name and my age, birthday, social security number, whose child I am and stupid things like that. (Well, these things aren't stupid, but you get my point.) I knew the stuff everybody knows about themselves, but I did not know who I really was. On social media and interacting with me from day to day, you might never guess I was having an identity crisis.

An identity crisis can occur way before a person reaches middle age. Lots of people think an identity crisis ensues when you hit forty-something and decide to try to prove you can keep up with the younger generation. That's one representation of an identity crisis, but it isn't the only one. An identity crisis happens when a person tries to navigate through life without knowing who they are and *whose* they are. It can happen at any age. In my early teens and all the way through my early twenties—from about sixteen until twenty-three—I had a continuous identity crisis. I did not know who I was. I searched for the answer for years and got frustrated when I couldn't find it where I was looking. Then one day, I found out who I was because I found out *whose* I was. By that, I mean I found God for real and I discovered I was His princess. I truly came to the realization, no matter how much I tried to fight it, I belonged to Him.

Let's start with the 'who' part. Who are you? Do you know who you are?

I had to come to a realization of who I am and that all the validation I wanted, needed and will ever need comes from God. I had to understand I am great because I was made in the image and likeness of someone great: God. I'm great not because of anyone else but Him.

The Bible clearly expresses this to us in the Scriptures. It's amazing how all the answers to life's questions are found in the Bible, but we don't bother to read our bibles. Part of the discovery of who I am and whose I am came from finding out what God had to say about me in His word. The Bible tells us God has made us wonderfully and deeply and uniquely complex. Knowing who you are becomes reality when you really understand that before you were even born, God knew who you were. Beyond that, the very hairs on your head are numbered and God knows them all.

So what does that mean to me, Adara? So what if He knows everything about me? What does that have to do with anything?

It has everything to do with everything, and I'll prove it to you. By the time you finish reading this book, it is my prayer you'll understand just how into you and concerned about you God really is. Before you were born, God knew every little detail about you, about your life and the twists and turns it would take. There is nothing about you that takes God by surprise...not even your flaws and mistakes. Every breath you take and move you make is accounted for with God. Taking this into consideration, since God knows you inside and out, your identity has everything to do with Him.

God knows you and loves you so much so, He gave up the most important person to Him: His son, Jesus. He knew you were going to make some mistakes and fall short. That's called sin. In the simplest of contexts, sin means to miss the mark or to have missed God's best. Not knowing who you are or not knowing whose you are is not God's best and will result in sin. It resulted in epic, tragic sin for me day after day after day because, although I was in the church, the church was not in me.

I had the religion down pat, but I had no relationship. I could sing all the songs and fake the funk Sunday morning during service, then turn around and hit a day party. I was a church girl, but not a God girl. Picture that, the pastor's daughter leading worship on Sunday morning and secretly the night before, she lit up her blunt. It doesn't matter who you are, whose biological child you are, how much money you have, how many friends you have... Unless you recognize your identity in Christ and you understand just how colossal and big the love of God is for you, you will feel so confused about your life and your existence. You will feel lost. I was lost, and that feeling of being lost with no hope of being found caused me to try to escape and cope with *that* reality.

The Bible is filled with verses which can help you explore and find your identity and, although I am going to list some of them throughout the pages of this book, I encourage you to check them out for yourself. Read and dissect them. Doing this helped me a lot.

It's been so funny to me that the one book I never really cared for has become the most valuable and essential part of my life. The Bible really does have the answers for every question and it holds the solid truth which is this: Jesus is the answer to all life's problems. He's the answer to your identity problem. He's the answer to your relationship problems, financial problems, etc. Whatever the problem...Jesus is the solution.

Everything won't magically be fixed overnight. That's a common misconception people have about Jesus. He's not an

Aladdin genie lamp you can rub and instantly get what you want or need, and then be on your way. A friendship and relationship with Jesus is give and take. Yes, you will be able to take what you need in this life, but you'll also have to give to Him. Giving to Jesus consists of giving quality time, energy, sincerity and effort. It consists of all the things you need to make any type of relationship or friendship work—and most definitely, last.

How can you be in a relationship—and have it work and actually last—with someone you don't know? That's right. You cannot do it. It will never, ever work.

How can you successfully have a growing, acting, thriving, healthy, vibrant relationship with a stranger? It is impossible.

The same is true of a relationship with Christ, and it's so simple. People have made Christianity out to be a complex religion when it's a really simple relationship. A relationship with Jesus will develop and grow the same way it would with a person: by spending time and getting to know the reality of who Jesus truly is. The reality of Jesus is so simple: He loves you! He loved you so much that He died on the cross to cover all the mistakes and slip ups you would have and He loves you enough to cover your identity crisis because your identity is found in Him. Once you believe in your heart and confess with your mouth that you believe in Jesus, and you believe your confession is real, you acknowledge the fact that you cannot make it far in life without Him and you make up in your mind to wholeheartedly choose Him, then your relationship with Him will start to develop and you will begin to uncover who He is and how He truly feels about you. You'll also begin to discover some things about yourself that are at the core of who you are and why you are here: YOUR IDENTITY. Many people, myself included, search for identity in people and places where it can never be found. Without Jesus, completion and wholeness will never truly be found or reached. It will never be found in other people, in things, in money, in careers...in anything but Jesus. I searched high and low, so trust me on this one. Identity is found in Jesus Christ.

I encourage everyone to do a study in your private time about what identity really means because again, you could have a crisis at any age if you don't know who you are and whose you are. The first scripture that began to unlock the mystery of my identity after I got saved for real (no more playing around in church) and I really began to search, was 2 Corinthians 5:17 (NLT) which says: *"therefore if any man be in Christ he is a new creature: old things have passed away, behold all things are become new."* Once, you choose to come to Christ, all the mistakes and bad choices you made before that choice get thrown out the window. Your record of wrongdoing, your record of sin, gets expunged. It can never be dug up or pulled out again.

Now the fact of the matter is people will try to bring up your faults and the things you've done, but the truth is there is *"no condemnation to him that is in Christ Jesus,"* as stated in Romans 8:1NLT. These Scriptures corroborate the idea that when you come to Christ, you get a fresh start, a do-over without the guilt or memory of what you used to be or what you used to do. No one can condemn you of what Christ already has cleansed you. No one can guilt you for what grace has excused you. You've got a new start and with a new start comes a chance to find out who you were all along. Those not so smart, not so great choices were not you. They were the result of you not knowing Jesus and not knowing *you*. Once you start to get to know Jesus, indeed, you will start to discover *you*, your choices, habits and desires. Even the types of mistakes you make will change. You see, you will still make many mistakes. Lord knows, I'm still falling, but I'm not falling into the same ditches I once fell into when I didn't know who I was. Whereas I once fell into the ditch of trying to be somebody I was not on social media, chasing after "Likes," now if I fall short, my identity doesn't fall apart in the process because I still know and I still have who I am. Your mistakes do not define you and you should not let them detain you.

You do not have to be a prisoner of regret or of any choices you've made once you've come to understand and admit they were wrong. The fact you've admitted to them being wrong is proof you are headed in the right direction. Admitting truly is the first step toward recovery, and a full, speedy recovery will only come through Jesus Christ. Nothing you've said or done is too hard for Jesus to forgive. He has covered everything. He has covered all my bases and yours too. Nothing and nobody can separate you from the love and saving grace of God through His son, Jesus Christ. One of the things I constantly tell myself when I start to look back over the things I've done and feel guilty is to say out loud, "My mistakes are not me!" Yes, I've made some not-so-great choices, but they don't define who I am as a person. Bad choices do not equate to me being a bad person. Who I am as a person is defined through Jesus and the unfailing love He has for me.

Sin causes you to be in way deep over your head. You'll catch yourself doing things you thought you would never do, trust me. Taking bottles of Hennessey to the face was not me. Rolling up blunts and taking pictures in little itty bitty, sexy clothes to post a picture just to get Likes and comments with heart eyes emoji was not me.

I thought those things were me. I tried to make them me. I smiled on camera like they were me, but it was never...me. It's funny because I can look at my old pictures and see how much hurt I was carrying. My eyes look dull and lifeless in most of those pictures. I barely smiled, mostly from trying to look seductive and sexy, but also because I was not happy, and rightfully so, because I had nothing to smile about or be happy about. Each and every time I did anything like that, I felt a void. I felt something missing. I never was fulfilled. I never got what I was looking for. Sin and not knowing who you really are will send you on a pricey, endless search in hopes of finding the answer that is right within your reach. In order to live a triumphant life and be secure in who you are, you must know who God is. I'm living better now because I learned.

Who I am has absolutely nothing to do with anybody else or what they do. You are you—not your family nor friends, and not your ancestry. Those are influential in helping you discover how you fit in this world, but they aren't you. Mom and Dad, brother and sister, auntie and uncle—the whole family is not you. Your interactions with them and relationships with them are not you.

You are you.

You will be like a hamster going aimlessly in a circle if you try to be anyone else but you, and this world will only be blessed by you if you give it *you*. You should give the world the wonderful, unique you God intended you to be because someone needs that and God thinks you are capable of being what they need. If He wanted duplicates, He would have made duplicates. Even twins and triplets are unique and different in their own ways. All of us are special and have a specific handprint from God on our lives.

You cannot be (and don't have to be) anyone else. That was a *big* lesson I had to learn. After all, my Dad is a pastor (hence, the affectionate nickname I've given him, "Pastor Daddy") and naturally I felt like I was living in his shadow. I felt like, to the world, I would be just Pastor Butler's daughter. It felt like I was nobody. That was the enemy's first substantial attack on me because I am somebody. The enemy wanted me to feel like a nobody because that would send me into a desperate whirlwind of trying to prove I was somebody, which was almost fatal because the very thing I was running from was actually my protection.

I got sick of everyone referring to me as Pastor Butler's daughter. Yes, I am his daughter, but I'm also my own person...or at least I wanted so badly to believe that. I was going to prove to my parents and to myself who I was without living in their shadow.

Part of the reason I resented being called Pastor Butler's daughter I was running from the calling on my life. I was wrestling with that; I did not want to become a duplicate of my father. I did not want ministry because I didn't want to be my dad and, foolishly and assumingly, I psyched myself into believing people would always see him when they saw me, especially in ministry. So I rebelled. I'm not talking about breaking a curfew by half an hour once or twice. I rebelled against everything I knew was right, and I did everything in my power to ensure and make clear we were nothing alike. I did it not because I was ungrateful or I didn't like my parents or my family. I love them. I did it because I was hurting. I was lost and confused and so upset that my parents decided on this ministry-based life for me. In my mind, they took away my chance to be "normal" when they decided to become pastors. (I'll explain more in the next chapter). I was furious I could never be normal, and somebody would pay the cost. I was hurt—and you know what they say: Hurt people hurt people. I was suffering and it wasn't fair. It wasn't until I really found God that I realized my suffering didn't have to be. I began to see how the enemy used self-esteem and a desire to belong against me. That was only one way he attacked me. There were several, but this was one of the biggest. I was fooled into feeling so small. I tried anything to make myself feel like something.

We can be so determined to do something that we don't see the dangers because we've made our decision and declared it final. I was going to have my own identity and that was final. I did not care about anyone around me. I ended up doing emotional damage not only to me, but also to my family. Your decisions never affect just you because none of us are an island nor ever truly alone. All of us, no matter how isolated we may feel, are connected to and affect someone else. The enemy wants you to feel isolated and alone so that you begin to move and operate under the premise that what you do won't affect anyone. It won't matter.

That's a bald-faced lie. Good, bad, or indifferent, the choices you make have an impact. The choices I made had an impact. My desperately wanting to be "normal" and known and "liked" had an impact. It impacted my family negatively. It caused unnecessary tension and drama in our home. It ate away at my self-esteem little by little. My romantic relationships reflected the way I felt about myself, and they were just as much of a mess as I was. I came to understand, looking back, that I couldn't function in my interactions with anybody on a deeper, long-lasting level nor get to know anyone else because I didn't even know me. I didn't know me, but I wanted people to know me and I created this image so people could know me.

I wanted people to know me independent of my churchy, pastor parents. I was about to be known alright. Attention and buzz were about to come my way and happen very quickly and they would be way, way more than I initially bargained for. That's usually what happens with sin and with falling into the enemy's trap. You always end up doing more and giving more away than you initially wanted to.

Mistakenly and under false reasoning, I felt like and thought I was nobody and that no one knew or could see the real me. I was not having that. The fact I have written a book about how I just wanted people to know of the real me and now, years later, all over the world people actually know of the real me is ironic. It's amazing how life changes, how we change, how situations change with God. I cannot scream this enough. I had *nothing* to do with getting to this point in my life. It has been all God. I was messed up. I was a hot mess. I was so desperate to define me independent of everyone around me. Yet today, when I am asked who I am, I can define myself because I now know *who* defines me.

I am a sinner who has been saved by grace. I am a woman who once was hurting for years, much like that woman with the blood issue and then, with just one touch from Jesus, like her, instantly I was made whole and made free. My issues were emotional and deep-seated heart issues, and God worked on me. I like to tell people I got a blood transfusion and the blood of Jesus Christ is what saved me. Jesus is a "Level5000" heart healer and life dealer.

If you follow my social media, you know that everything with me is Level 5000. 5,000 happens to be my favorite number. It's a significant number because Jesus took a little bit of nothing (two fish and five loaves of bread) and made it into something that was able to touch 5,000 people. That's precisely what He did for me. He took away the feelings of incompletion and void and replaced them with something great: Him. At times, I wish I could go back in time and erase all the things I did, but then I wouldn't have been able to write this book or share with you how I've gotten so strong. Finding out who I am has been liberating; it has freed me, but it wouldn't have happened had I not been bound and a prisoner to my emotions and the burdens I was carrying.

But before we even get into the nitty gritty, before I open up to you in vast detail about how I did all this crazy stuff to like myself and ultimately ended up hating the girl I saw staring back at me in the mirror, which was way more than I bargained for, before I really ultra shock you with some secrets about me, let's go back to where it all began. Like all good stories, including the story of mankind, everything is always good, real good...in the beginning.

Chapter 2

Identity Crisis Times a Million

Everywhere I go to this day, everywhere we go, *somebody* knows my father, my mother or both of them. I promise this isn't an exaggeration, like my captions on Instagram, and I'm rolling both eyeballs as I write this.

My parents just "know people." They are well-liked and respected. Long Island, New York—Freeport, Baldwin, Roosevelt, Uniondale, Hempstead and the surrounding areas—is kind of small, figuratively speaking, because somebody knows somebody that knows somebody that knows somebody. I come from a huge family; people know us all. My family includes a long lineage of musicians and preachers so you might think I would have gotten the memo a long time ago that I am to be a preacher, too.

Musician? Eh, not so much. I can hold a little tune in the shower under God's grace with the water drowning out my off-key notes, but I'm not a singer. My younger siblings, Kim and DJ, got that anointing, and I celebrate them. It should have clicked that I would be ministering and preaching, and that I could never get away from that because it is in my blood line.

I did *not* want to be a preacher. Nobody in their right mind wants to be a preacher, at least not a *real* preacher. It's not glamorous, and it is hard work. The real, unadulterated Gospel is not popular. People have lost their lives to preach and live this life. The average teenage/young adult woman does not just wake up and decide she wants to preach the Gospel. This young woman whose book you are reading did not want to live this life. I did not want this. Preaching the Gospel has been all God; I had other plans for my life. I intentionally and purposely ran the opposite way because I knew what this would require of me and I did not think it was cool nor normal for a regular girl, despite feeling the tugging and the calling from a very young age.

I was an extremely peculiar child. Like most girls, I had Barbie® dolls and baby dolls, but unlike most girls, I was "playing church" with them. I would line them up and raise their arms like they were receiving prayer, then pray over them. I had many shut-ins with my dolls who were delivered many times. Barbie®

was baptized when I took a bath and wrapped up in a towel just like me.

I was different. From a young age, I was aware of the things of church and of God, and they came effortlessly to me. Unfortunately, as I grew into my preteen and teenage years, I began to desire the things of God less. They were not "fun." I saw the worldly things people did, and *that* seemed like fun.

I would later discover those things really are not that much fun—and they come with a cost.

I went astray. I moved away from my Christian upbringing and from the principles my parents instilled in me long before I took even my first drink, getting wasted to the point of no recollection at a mere age 16. The seed for losing my way started to grow in the year 2000 at roughly nine and a half—of course, Mom was already privileged to this information—when my father sat us all down in the living room one evening and told us we were leaving the church we attended because "God told him to become a pastor."

On the outside, I was silent and calm and just listened to what was being said by my parents. On the inside I boiled and screamed. If I thought I could shake my father and demand he come to his senses without the threat of getting a whooping, I would have. This man had lost his mind. In my mind, in that moment, my father singlehandedly ruined my life. We were already not normal because *nobody* in my class went to church as much as we did. People didn't understand when I declined parties and sleepovers—my parents were downright *different*.

The older I get, the more thankful I am for them not only being different, but also being obedient to God. In some ways, their ways literally saved my life. I've suffered some traumatic things in my life, but none of it during my formative years because my parents had wisdom and discernment and did not let us do whatever we wanted. I see that now, but as a child, I often resented them for it. I challenged them and rebelled because I felt they were ruining my life and keeping me in a box. They did keep me in a box, but that "box" was my protection. That "box" would help me find my way back after becoming a prodigal princess. It was divine protection. It would prove to save my life, my future and my destiny.

When Daddy told us he was becoming a pastor, I was beyond furious. I thought, *Who the heck asked you to do that?! You always have some great idea for the family to do.* Of course, being the Level 5000 smart girl I am, I kept these thoughts to myself so I didn't lose my lips, but I was boiling mad. Life couldn't get worse. First, it was growing up without a television and now this???

I already wasn't up on the latest and greatest shows on TV because we didn't have one in our household. (Actually, we had TV; we just did not have cable, and we didn't get cable until I was thirteen.) I didn't get hip to all the shows everyone loved, like *The Cosby Show* and *The Fresh Prince of Bel Air,* and all of the cartoons and movies most people still love, until my early teen years. I grew up watching VHS cassettes of Disney movies, *Blue Clues, Story Keepers* and *Veggie Tales*. We weren't poor so it wasn't that we could not afford cable. My dad got rid of cable so that we could spend time together as a family and with God.

His theory was actually right.

Judging by how much time kids spend in front of technology and their TVs, iPads, and whatever else they have today, Pastor Daddy was definitely on to something. Still, at ten years old, I wasn't interested in trading cartoons for God, but what could I do? Nothing. Except throw out my vegetables when nobody was looking, my silent expression of rebellion.

I was 100% not in favor of his decision. It kicked off an intense internal war that would last for years, and that would contribute to me becoming the Prodigal Princess.

Let me tell you what I mean.

All I wanted was to be "normal." At age twenty-five, as I'm writing my first book, I see I've always been normal in the sense that nothing was wrong with me. At the same time, I've always been peculiar or different because I have a unique purpose and calling...and nothing is wrong with that.

Truthfully, to be downright 100 with you, I just wanted to fit in. Most girls grow up with dozens of friends and playmates, but I didn't have that. I was never the super popular girl everyone loved. My best friends were my sisters, my cousins and friends from church.

Until fifth grade when I met my best friend, Imani.

Before that, I had few "friends." Our closest friends who were not family were our neighbors, but even that interaction was limited. The children on our block came to visit and play in our backyard. We had a huge swing set and clubhouse fort. We were not allowed to sleep over any and everybody's house, go hang out unsupervised, and do whatever we wanted. The closest I came to attending parties before age 16—when I began to sneak out—was family and church functions.

To many, this seems overbearing and too much. Shoot, it seemed that way to me at the time, but the older I get, the more I appreciate that my parents set boundaries. We grew up differently—not isolated, but not exposed to just anything. We were not exposed to just any and everybody. As far gone as I eventually was, as wayward as I became, there still were some things I never got exposed to, and for that I'm thankful. My parents raised us the right way, the way I plan to raise my children. I'm thankful I had parents with good enough sense to be not my peer, but rather my parent. They had good enough sense to protect me to the best of their ability and they will forever have a gold star in my hall of fame.

I couldn't see back then that my parents were trying to shield me from the lures of the world. I thought they were overprotective and mean, and that they lived to make my life boring. You couldn't tell me my folks didn't sleep well at night knowing I was bored. But the opposite was true. They cared for me deeply and wanted to protect me. They understood their role as godly parents was to raise me in the fear of the Lord and to protect me, but their protection came with restrictions and I didn't understand. Lacking tons of friends, not being the popular girl and not having certain "freedoms" other kids had caused me to resent my parents and church and vow that when I was old enough to take care of myself, I would do everything they never let me do. I would make friends and do all the things I thought normal people did when hanging out with their friends.

I equated frivolous activities with friendship because I was immature. The immature me vowed that as soon as I was "grown" (which, in my head, meant age eighteen), I would come and go as I pleased. I would party and do all the things I wanted to do. I began plotting how I would assert my adulthood and individuality from my preteen years. I would establish myself as a person independent of my parents. I would live my life.

If it involved church or God, I would have nothing to do with it.

Well, as you can see, I didn't get very far with that immature mindset. Even in the midst of my epically sinful lifestyle, God's grace and hand of protection was on me and over me. His plan has always and will always supersede my plan.

Eventually, I started to feel daring and courageous. I didn't have to wait until eighteen. I began to try to assert my "adulthood" about age fifteen. What I didn't realize, although I did "grown people" things, I was still a child and had much to learn. I was about to learn some hard lessons, lessons that molded me into the woman I am today. Although my quest for my identity began to unfold at age fifteen, ten years later, it is still unfolding and changing, completely opposite what I thought it was or would be.

Chapter 3

Where Christ is Management....

There's Crisis Management

In the summer of my fifteenth year, my body started to go through big changes. Yes, I was a late bloomer. I'm still blooming, wishing on a Popeye's fried chicken leg and a prayer that I might fill out just a little bit more. I'm about one hundred thirty pounds soaking wet. I have grown to love the body I am in, but I didn't always love it. I came to love it because I'm stuck with it.

When my body began changing, I was a hot tamale, honey! I was fifteen and so glad finally to have started to blossom. By then, I had my menstrual cycle and all that good stuff, but now, at fifteen, my hips got a little wider, I became a little more shapely, as my "blessed assurance" expanded (read between the lines) and I had hair down my back I could flip. I became aware I was female. I was, by biological construct and by physical attributes, a *woman*.

A fire started to ignite within, I started feeling myself and I made the first major decision that would change my life. I gave away my most prized treasure.

I gave away my virginity.

That's right. I got my freak on at fifteen.

So young, and so impressionable. I didn't know anything, but you couldn't tell me that. The lures of the world in a sex-driven society, despite my parents' warnings, had made such an impression on me that I thought, *it's just sex...everyone does it.* Since the girls at school did it and talked about it and their boyfriends loved them, mine would love me forever if we did it, too.

Did I forget to mention I had a boyfriend behind Daddy and Mommy's back? With all the boundaries and protections, that rebellious seed in me took full root. I had a boyfriend behind their backs, and at fifteen, I lost my virginity.

I knew the implications of sex outside of marriage. I knew it was sin. My parents gave me "the talk" more than once, but as you can see, that didn't stop me. I was so curious about the world they tried to shield me from that I ran toward it.

Everything my parents warned me about sex came true, although not all at once. Everything, from heartbreak to unplanned pregnancy. It all came true.

No, your eyes are not fooling you. Little Ms. Encourager, Little Ms. Preacher—the woman *so* strong and *so* empowered, the one whose father is well known in the community and pastors a decent-sized, rapidly growing church—got pregnant outside of marriage in her teen years.

You can pick your jaw up. I'm survived and I'm still saved. And no, I don't have a child. Well, that's not exactly accurate...I *do* have a child, a daughter who would be about eight and half or so and probably full of fire and attitude just like me. I have a daughter. I never met her. She resides in heaven, but I'll get to that later.

That first time I had sex opened a door, a Pandora's Box, if you will. Once that door opened, little by little, other doors opened me up to other things. I thought sex played a part in who I was. Not knowing my true identity, I thought my body played a part in my identity and if I used it right, I would indeed be perceived a woman. I thought my shape and looks and knowing how to make myself look appealing and sexy made me a woman.

That was lie, a worldly lie the enemy fed me.

At fifteen, because of what I saw in media and at school, these lies were my misconceptions and these misconceptions carried me well into my early adult years and the onset of social media.

When I started "bumpin' and thumpin'," as my older sister Qiana calls it, I was still a child, and like all wayward children, I eventually would have to face the consequences of going out on my own and doing adult things.

I regret losing my virginity for so many reasons. It wasn't romantic like it was on TV. I had to sneak out to do it, and I felt conviction immediately after. I felt terrible for giving away my treasure to someone who did not deserve it. Deep down, I knew that had this person really loved me like he said he did, sex wouldn't even have come up. Still, it felt good, so I kept him close and doing so gave me a sense of power I equated to my identity as a woman. I kept engaging in sex before marriage, sneaking around my pretty tight schedule for school and extracurricular activities. I became skilled—pretty much had my Ph.D.—in sneaking out in the middle of the night while everyone slept. Guilt always hovered over me. Moreover, I knew I was breaking God's heart. My sin and this lifestyle I was living was not what He wanted from me...or for me.

But I was selfish. It was all about me.

After all, that's what sin does to you, right? It makes you think of only you, what satisfies and benefits you, and it makes you completely blind to how your actions affect those around you— or perhaps you know how your actions could affect others, but you really don't care. That was a big motto of mine for all the years I was in my mess. My motto was "I don't care about it."

Whenever my parents lovingly tried to tell me I didn't have go down the road I was going, my answer was, "I don't care." Deep down inside, I actually did care. Deep down, I knew I was troubled, but a little trouble wasn't that big of a deal, right? It would go away, right?

Wrong!

Trouble is like a balloon. It expands and expands and expands some more until it reaches its maximum and then BOOM...the balloon has busted. My balloon busted all right and the pieces went everywhere. Finding my identity in Christ was the way my pieces came back together and became a brand new, shiny balloon—the cool kind you get on special occasions. It was a process, though, a processed birthed out of crisis.

You see, earlier I mentioned you could have an identity crisis way before you reach middle age if you really don't know who you are. I did. I had a crisis, a repeated nightmare when I tried to run away from who I was called to be and from what I was called to do because I thought my destiny wasn't normal. Had I embraced the calling on my life I wouldn't have tried to be an adult and do adult things before an appropriate time.

I had an innate fear of never having my own voice and always living in my parents' shadow. It was a valid concern. We all should desire to be unique, not be a direct duplicate of someone else, since that is how God made us.

What was not valid was my fear that if I fully chose Jesus, ministry and life would never be "fun." What does "fun" even mean? For goodness' sake, sometimes sleeping is fun. How dumb was it to feel like I was missing out on something that can't even truly be defined? Fun means different things to different people, and I learned what fun truly meant for me.

Fun is whatever you make it when you are secure and comfortable with who you are.

I've learned the *hard* way, the unnecessarily painful way, that drinking and smoking yourself into oblivion and an upset stomach that lasts for days at a time really is not that much fun in the end. It was fun to me in the moment, but at the end, I never felt great or fulfilled. I thought if I just tried enough times, if I could make a habit of that lifestyle. I could learn to love the "turn up" lifestyle, and it would be fun. I thought I would be able to put the idea of ministry and preaching behind me.

That was super dumb of me.

Running from God and purposely going the wrong way was flat out dumb. No matter what anyone says, running from God was NOT FUN. It was the exact opposite. It was painful.

I've done some dumb things in my time, but I'm thankful to have grown from them. The older I get, the more I see exactly how I got sucked into the web of deceit, identity crisis, frustration, pain, etc. The enemy can and will play upon whatever area of your life in which you are insecure or not strong. He will use whatever you have not surrendered to the Lord against you. If it's your emotions, you'd better believe he will come against your emotions. If it's your self-esteem, you'd better believe he will strategically attack that. I can only speak on things I know and have experienced firsthand. The enemy crept into my space in several ways; lack of confidence and self-esteem was just one way. It's amazing—and somewhat funny, ironically—no matter how many people tell you that you are beautiful or special, those are just empty words until you believe you are. I always heard I was a "bright girl" or I was "so pretty," and yet I believed the tiny whisperings of the enemy who said otherwise. That is part of the reason I sought validation in people.

If you ride off the approval and appreciation of people instead of God, you'll seek after it always. I learned I cannot please everyone and I would kill myself trying. I thought sure if people liked me, I would be complete. I thought I could identify myself through some sort of approval and validation from people. That was the stupidest logic ever. In fact, that line of thinking made things ten times worse. Identity never has anything do with anyone or anything else but Christ and Christ alone.

I had to learn how to be happy with me and to accept me for me, not for anyone else, but for *me*. It was a hard lesson. Chasing after validation on social media after not getting the fulfillment I wanted out of my relationships and chasing after wholeness in people and in things are what really broke me, but there's good news.

I like giving good news. Maybe that's why I'm now in love with the Gospel of Jesus Christ and can preach it. I think I love it because it's all Good News. After hearing bad news several times, you need some good news.

So here's my good news. Are you ready for this? Brokenness is the perfect place for God to operate.

He's like a surgeon who specializes in brokenness, and He did. The Surgeon performed open heart surgery on me after my fall and collapse. I'd been running from Him for so long when what I was desired was right there in my brokenness. In my pain, I learned my identity.

I AM ROYALTY.

I AM GOD'S PRINCESS.

THIS IS MY IDENTITY.

It took many nights of fake fun and feeling incomplete, and it took crumbling and crashing to understand the real Adara is a princess. She's a gem. She belongs to a King. I am royalty because I belong to The King.

You too are royalty. YOU also belong to a King...*the* King. The King named Jesus.

The super awesome thing I learned about my identity was that I would grow and blossom and I wouldn't have to hurt myself in the process. I would go through changes without having to compromise or change myself. I learned I was allowed to be a masterpiece—God's masterpiece—and yet, a work in progress. I will never get everything correct, and that it is okay.

There's so much pressure from society to be perfect. Society teaches you that you have to have the perfect body, the perfect hair, the latest clothes and be liked by everyone. Society teaches us wrongly. You don't have to be liked by everyone. If I may let you in on a secret...You won't be.

At your absolute best, you still won't be enough to people, but you always have been and always will be enough to Christ. That's the whole premise of His love. His love is unconditional, meaning it's there, no matter what. Your identity is yours, no matter what has happened in the past or is happening right now. Why? Because your identity in Christ is yours no matter when you choose Him. The Bible tells us once you've accepted Christ, you are God's child. In John 1:12-13 NLT, it states *"but to all who believed him and accepted him, he gave the right to become children of God. They are reborn—not with a physical birth resulting from human passion or plan, but a birth that comes from God."*

The being re-born part is the key. Rebirth happens as we receive salvation, and it's not something that has to happen over and over again. Salvation is not membership to a gym where you have to pay fees over and over, then renew your membership. Salvation costs you $0.00. It's a decision to have a change of heart, a turn of heart and to exercise a daily lifestyle. Once it happens and takes root, you are free to live in peace—for Christ and with Christ. You are beginning your journey of walking in your true identity because you have returned back to whom you belonged all along. That's the nature of true identity in a nutshell. It's being aligned with and to whom you belong.

It's kind of like when a puppy is lost, then returned to its owner and rightful home. The puppy didn't stop being a puppy while it was lost. It never stopped being the owner's puppy, even though it was a stray puppy up for grabs by anyone. It could have been kidnapped, stolen or killed, all because it somehow lost its way, but someone was nice enough to sacrifice and make a trip to bring the lost puppy home to its owner. Jesus Christ is the person, figuratively and spiritually speaking, who was nice enough to bring me—the lost, shaggy, crusty, puppy who lost her way—home to her owner, back to God.

So the underlying question and my question to you is, who are you? Do you know who you are? Do you know *whose* you are?

Tough questions to answer, huh? I get it. They were tough for me too...when I didn't know.

I will never forget one night when I was headed out to the club as usual—half-naked in a skimpy outfit about to hit the streets after I pre-gamed just enough to get a buzz. My father stopped me on the way out the door. He said "Adara, who are you?" To this day, Pastor Daddy has a way of asking that one question that will stop you dead in your tracks and change your whole thought process. I know for a fact God was speaking to me through him because I DID NOT KNOW.

Pride, frustration, rage, anger, hurt and guilt all led me to answer with a sarcastic, nasty answer. I puffed up my chest and coldly, sarcastically answered, "I'm Pastor Darren E. Butler Sr.'s daughter. No more, no less." Then, I grabbed my change of flats, my personal bottle of whatever I was drinking that night and stomped out the door, slamming it behind me so hard the wreath on the door fell off.

On the inside, I was crying out and my father could see it. I didn't know who I was. I thought I could make myself be this sexy, cool, I-don't-care-about-life, I'm-just-here-to-have-fun girl, but I couldn't. The more I tried, the more I hurt myself. I was hurting from not knowing who I was and thinking the things that happened to me defined who I was. They didn't, but this was something I would discover and be liberated from much later.

For years, I carried guilt, anger, hurt and rage because of choices I made that went horribly wrong. Selfishly, I looked to blame others. For years, I was bitter toward my family and church because I made a huge choice based on what I assumed would happen to my family and my church family, a conscious choice that would prove to be a huge mistake. It would lead to more mistakes and more poor choices. It began a cycle, a domino effect that would last for a very long time until I got healing.

I thought my mistakes defined me and that kept me in emotional bondage for so long. I rebelled against the things of God and hardened my heart against my parents and church when I found myself pregnant at seventeen and faced with the hard choice of whether to keep my baby.

Yup, pregnant.

You're shocked. Imagine how I felt. I didn't believe it either.

Condoms were used every time I had sex so how did this happen? Like sex education teaches and my parents tried to teach me: condoms are not 100% guaranteed. I now know just how very accurate that is. One time the condom failed and as a result, I was pregnant. I knew right away, too, but I took about seven different tests in Level 5000 shock and disbelief. Each test said the same thing. Over and over and over again, the test read positive.

Pregnant.

Got 'em!

Never in my wildest dreams did I imagine myself in these shoes. Me?! Never. I turned my nose up at the girls who wobbled around junior high and high school. Little did I know I would soon find myself just like those girls. I was not mature enough for sex at the time I started having it. My first encounter with humility and real life came in the eleventh grade. Most eleventh grade girls are prepping for SATs and prom. I was prepping to hide this problem from my parents for as long as I could. I didn't know how to tell them.

Teen pregnancy rocked my world and turned it upside down. It wasn't just that I was pregnant. It wasn't just that I was getting sick and my body was changing. It wasn't just that I started gaining inexplicable weight, and my hormones were so crazy, I cried over the stupidest things. It was because I was the daughter of a well-known pastor whose church was growing steadily. People looked to my father for guidance; they trusted him. If and when my secret, my slip up, got out, who would trust a guy who couldn't control his own kids? Who would continue to attend his church and sit under his teaching?

I thought I would ruin my father's ministry and my family's lives for sure if I had this baby. I thought my parents would be so disgusted and disown me. I thought my father might kill my boyfriend, and I didn't want that either. (He definitely would come to have an effective prison ministry later down the line, but I didn't want it to start out of this situation.)

Most important to me was my dad's heart. As much as I despised the fact he had accepted the call to pastor a church and in doing so, took away my chance to be a normal girl, I still didn't want to hurt him. Having my baby would hurt him and it would cost him. This situation would break his heart. I was the worst daughter ever and everything was entirely my fault.

I really and truly have to let out a good, hearty, knee-slapping laugh sometimes at the lies I allowed the enemy to feed me. I chuckle at how fearful and overly dramatic I was, unnecessarily so. Fear caused me to panic and try to fix my mistake. What I didn't know was that my parents knew what was up. They knew from jump street.

Parents really aren't dumb. They might be crazy if they are like mine, but never, ever dumb. Parents know their children. Our parents mirror God in the respect that they know the people they've created just as God knows who He has created.

Fear of what I had done and knowledge of the consequences for what I had done caused me to try to figure out all the ways this could go and find the easiest way out.

Now, who does that sound like? Good ole' Adam and Eve! Picture that. I acted just like Adam and Eve. It makes sense, though, and proves the Bible is right—in case you were wondering if the words in the Bible are true. The Bible says all have sinned and fallen short of the glory of God, fallen short of His glorious standard for living, according to Romans 3:23. This sinning and falling short started with Adam and Eve.

History always repeats itself, even biblically speaking. In this day and time, I did the same thing as Adam and Eve once did in the Bible. I did exactly what I was told not to do. Then, when it blew up in my face, I hid my sin and hid behind it, afraid.

In my head, I was in panic mode. I hid the pregnancy because I was afraid, then I lied when asked about it. Even though I was showing—because I'm very tiny—I lied and lied. I avoided people while wrestling with my choice. If I kept the baby, all that was good about my life would be destroyed. If I didn't keep it and quietly handled it, everything could continue to be the way it was. Nothing bad would happen, and nobody would get hurt.

Eleventh grade...unwed...seventeen years young...with college around the corner...five months with kid and starting to show—do I, or do I not, keep my baby?

Decisions, oh, decisions. At almost or maybe even twenty-something weeks pregnant, undoubtedly and unmistakably *way* past the time you are legally allowed to make a "choice," I made mine. After countless crying nights, still in shock I was even in this predicament, out of fear of all I mentioned above, I made my choice, and it was *my* choice. The choice was left to me because the father of my baby did not want a baby. We were not even on the best of terms relationship-wise. We were on and off, and at the time I discovered I was pregnant, we were off, so I did what I felt at the time was best for everyone...except me. I chose what I thought was the least costly option, which ironically was the most costly monetarily, but I convinced myself it was for the best and that I would live and get past it.

I did *not* keep my baby.

I terminated my pregnancy.

Yup, I had an abortion, but keep reading, as I promise my story gets even better. I'm just scratching the surface. You'll soon see that was not even the worst of it. The actual procedure was only the beginning of a long, cold, lonely and guilty walk of pain, a walk that sent me on a quest to find out who I was and who I was not, to look for answers, high and low.

Literally...*high* and low.

The good news, as I said before—and I love good news because it makes me happy—is I'm no longer on that long, lonely search. I now know who I am. I know *whose* I am. That's how I'm able to write this book and open up to you about everything I've gone through. I've come to terms with the fact that yes, I've done some things and some things were done to me that were not good, but neither of those are not a part of my identity. If you are reading this and struggling with identity, please understand you are not alone. I was there. Identity Crisis was the street on which I lived. I am proof, however, there is hope and an answer.

I have more to tell you, but right now, I want you to know when you lock into the source of your identity, your search will be over. At the end of a few of the chapters in this book, there are prayers I share for dealing with the struggles or strongholds discussed in that chapter. So here is the first prayer. It's for you and anyone else struggling with identity, with not belonging, with regrets, with wondering if you are more than the bad things that have happened to you. My answer—and more importantly,

God's answer—is yes, you are. God loves you and His love covers everything. His love is where your identity starts. His love starts with the love of Jesus Christ.

This is a prayer you can pray regarding identity:

Lord Jesus, I admit I've fallen short of your best for my life. I admit that things have not gone the best way they could and I know that's because something has been missing. I've searched for what's missing and have yet to find it. I believe in my heart, You are what is missing and I need You. Now, in this moment, in my heart, I invite You in.

I ask You into my heart and into my life. I believe You came here to the earth, that You died on the Cross for my sins, that You rose from the dead and that in You is where my identity lies. I believe with my heart and confess with my mouth that You are Lord and King, and everything about me is beautiful when I am in You.

In your name I pray,

Amen.

Well, how easy was that? In two minutes flat, you started your journey to finding your identity, and I'm willing to bet a dollar ('cause that's all I have to give you right now), you felt this sort of peace, didn't you? I know you did. That's the love of God and that's how instantaneously He moves when He is invited.

If this was your very first time praying a prayer like this, or if you re-prayed and are coming back to Jesus, CONGRATULATIONS! Not only did you accept Jesus Christ as

Lord and Savior, you began the journey to finding out who and whose you are, and you're on the right track.

I'm not going to tell you everything about life instantly changes and gets better. It could, but often, it does not. To make you believe it always happens that way would be lying to you. However, it does get easier and you will start to find out who you are.

The next step is to get a Bible. My suggestion and go-to in terms of bibles is the New Believer's Study Bible, New Living Translation, or NLT, version. Get one and begin to read it. Read your Bible every day and pray every day. The same way you just prayed that prayer is the same way you can talk to God—in your words, in your language. In open, sincere honesty with Him, and He will talk to you. I wish and pray you truly uncover your identity and who you are as a unique individual in Jesus Christ.

If you were already a believer and follower of Jesus, perhaps this prayer was indirectly for you, too. I pray this prayer served as a reminder of the team for which you signed up. I pray this reminded you of when and where you discovered that your identity lies in Jesus Christ.

Love, *Adara*

Chapter 4

Purpose? What's That?!?

My favorite Scripture of all time has been and always will be Romans 8:28 NLT which states *"all things work together for the good of those who love the Lord and are called according to His purpose."*

I've loved this Scripture since I can remember reciting and recalling scripture when I was young. This Scripture always made me feel good. I guess you could say reading it always provided some sort of soothing whenever I felt any sort of way except happy. So it's always been a "good Scripture" to me, but when I really, like for real, for real, uncovered the true essence of what this Scripture meant, it became that much more my favorite. It really uncovered some mysteries for me and what I really was longing and searching for.

Purpose, according to *Merriam Webster's Dictionary* is "the reason for which something is done or created or for which something exists." Secondly, in verb form, it is defined as "to have as one's intention or objective." In other words, purpose is defined as the point of why something was created or has come to be and as the aim or plan of something.

For a long, long time, I did not know my purpose nor did I understand it. I knew what I liked to do. This may come as a surprise considering I'm writing this book, but then again, maybe not. I knew what I wanted to do. I knew what I could do, but I did not know what I was *supposed* to do.

Well, that's not exactly true. I take that back. (I think I'm allowed to do that, right? Okay, good. I take that back.)

I knew what I was supposed to do, but what I was supposed to do wasn't what I wanted to do. Because it wasn't what I wanted, I fought it and that led me to feeling lost and confused about my purpose.

It's kind of like knowing you have a destination to get to that you've never been to, but having a precise map in front of you from someone who has been there. Then, someone comes along and tells you they know a better or quicker way. Instead of going with the directions from the trusted person, you go with the directions from the person with the possible shortcut. That's what I did. I took the shortcut to my purpose, thinking I'd found a quicker, smoother way to do what I just *knew* God wanted me to do with my life. It was what I wanted, I would be doing something constructive (whatever that means) and I would be happy. All would be well.

Except...that didn't work.

My plan was an epic fail. It was a fail because it was not God's plan; it was mine. The Bible tells us in Proverbs 16:9 NLT, "*we can make our plans, but the Lord determines our steps.*"

If only I had respected and understood this from the get-go, I would have understood that no matter how many plans I made or what purpose I had for myself, God's purpose for me was bigger and more powerful. I didn't. I was so set on doing my life my way. After all, it was *my* life, man! Why should anyone, even God, tell me how to live it? Shouldn't my life be how I planned and purposed it?

Naturally, the answer would be yes, except my life—and yours too—doesn't belong to me or to you, and if our lives don't belong to us, then man, I guess our plans for our lives don't really matter in the overall scheme of things. What we want is trivial in comparison to what God wants for us, trivial in comparison to His purpose for us.

Ugh!

I know I busted your plan bubble. Mine got busted, too. You'll survive.

I survived, and I learned there's a reason why my plan didn't work out nor did it prove to be what I wanted or needed. The reason is my plan was all about my selfish will. It was centered on me. Me, me and more me. There was little to no room for God because there was so much of me. No wonder I was drowning. I was drowning in me and what I wanted for me, and there was no point or purpose in that.

The thing about purpose sometimes, at least with God's purpose, not ours, is that many times, it is not what we want for ourselves. But God's purpose is not about us, it's about what God wants. My conflict and struggle with purpose came not because I had no clue why I was here; it came because I had some inkling and clue, but I didn't want that for myself or understand why it had to be that way. I knew deep, deep down on the inside I was going to be a preacher someday, but that is not what Adara wanted.

What young woman wakes up one day and decides she wants to stand up in the pulpit or behind the sacred desk and declare the Gospel? Not this one. I was not interested. As far as I was concerned, my purpose in life was to be a high school teacher, help children, be a good person and yes, love God. In my head, I was convinced if I did these things, I would fulfill my purpose and I would be happy.

Boy, oh boy, was I wrong. Dead wrong.

As I would learn, your occupation or career choice is not your purpose. It can play a part in your purpose, however, it is *not* your purpose. Don't worry, I'm going break it all down for you— the notion of purpose and what not, and I'll use the Scriptures to corroborate my point, like any good preacher or teacher does— or parents like mine did. (They had Bible for everything, even down to chore distribution in our house. If there is Bible to prove why I had to do chores every Saturday to Gospel music blasting through the house, there definitely is Bible to back up the true meaning of purpose, and there is.) Let's first look at purpose by God's definition. Let's look at what it is and then we will examine examples of it at work in our lives. You ready? Cool, let's do it.

Purpose, in a Godly sense, is found in many Scripture verses. In the remaining few pages of this chapter, we will walk through a few that helped me and prayerfully, they will help you. "What was God's purpose for creating me?" may be a question you've asked yourself. If you have, that is good! You should wonder and want to know why you were born. There should be something inside of you that wants to know exactly what is the point of God waking you up every day. That point is your purpose.

Unfortunately, so many people walk around unhappy and unfulfilled simply because they don't know God nor the reason He allowed them to be born. The circumstances under which you came to the earth, whether your family situation at the time of your birth was good or bad, happy or sad, don't matter. You matter, and you have a reason for being born. There is a purpose and point for why you came into existence. I don't care what has or hasn't been said, what has or hasn't been done. YOU matter and YOU have a purpose.

As a matter of fact, you have multiple purposes. That is, you have more than one purpose. We all have multiple purposes, some which are similar and then, we also have our individual purpose. Let's look at the common purposes we all have first. There are two I want to share with you.

Your first purpose above all else is to bring glory to God. That's the first and foremost reason you and I exist. That's the first reason we were born, to show and prove how awesome God is. Your very existence, your creation, achieves this. Until you acknowledge and understand this, you'll walk around aimlessly. I know because I did. I thought I could coast through life and "do me" because it was "my life."

Womp, womp, womp.

Pull out the violins. Wrong answer.

Our lives are not our own. The air we breathe isn't ours because we didn't create it. God did. Everything we have and everything we are belongs to God. Therefore, our lives are intended to be lived in such a way that the greater being in us, who is actually Him, is seen by others. We are destined by design to be a great example of how good God is.

The Bible tells us in Exodus 9:16 ESV, God said *"...for this purpose I have raised you up, to show you my power, so that my name may be proclaimed in all the earth."* The Bible also tells us, in Matthew 5:16 NLT, we are *"to let our light shine in front of other people so they see our good works and in turn give glory to God."* Another passage found in 1 Corinthians 10:31 ESV says, *"Whether you eat or drink, or whatever you do, do all to the glory of God."* These Scriptures tell us everything we say and do should be productive and lead to others being able to recognize God on the inside of us, drawing them to Him.

Understanding this leads us to examine our motives and motivation for what we do. Why do we do or not do things? Everything we put effort, time and attention into should be centered around and aimed at God. Colossians 3:23 ESV says it better than I ever could because it so clearly says, *"Whatever you do, work heartily, as for the Lord and not for men."* It is evident our careers, jobs, hobbies, interests, etc. are not the issue. The issue is our motive for choosing them. Unless the motive and motivation is God, it will not be profitable, enjoyable, meaningful and certainly, not purposeful. Since purpose comes from God, purpose will only be achieved when our choices are aimed at honoring God.

So many people are walking around in turmoil and defeat, in anger and hurt and confusion, feeling unfulfilled because they simply don't know—and don't know that they don't know—they have been designed and put on this earth to live in a way that brings honor to God.

This is at the root of everything. It is meaningful and the way we connect to Him. We connect to God through our lives and how we live for Him. So, our first purpose is to live a life that is honorable to God. Everything we do, say and even think should be aimed at pleasing God, proving to Him and showing others how much we love Him. It should also be aimed at convincing and proving to others through action how awesome He is, and how grateful we are for our existence as well as His.

It's kind of like going hard for your favorite player or the best player on a team, the player you believe is the real MVP. You want everyone to know how incredible that player is. Everybody may not believe in the team you are rooting for nor believe in that player, but that's both okay and irrelevant to you because that player is *your* choice for MVP. You know what that player is capable of. You've studied the ins and outs of their strategies and how he or she moves. You know everything about them. You are a real fan. You have a deep appreciation and love for who they are as well as what they do.

Well, living in purpose *on purpose* for God is exactly the same.

By living out our purpose, we as believers or followers of Christ, those who think of God as the real MVP, are telling others we love and appreciate Him for who He is and for what He does for us. By living in a way that is holy—reflective of God—we show others how much He means to us, and in doing so, can and should make them want to live for Him, too. We are ambassadors, talent scouts, a recruitment team for the Kingdom of God. By living out our first purpose, we draw people in and make them believe in and want to share in our love for the MVP. Our love and devotion brings glory and honor to God. If we live this way, we are in fact living in purpose and living out purpose. So that's purpose number one—to bring glory to God with all that we have, all that we are and all that we do.

There's more, so keep reading.

The second purpose we all commonly have is to live productively and wholesomely in such a way that we are a light and a hope to others and we service a greater purpose *beyond ourselves.* No matter how big or small a task we have, we are supposed to do it "as unto God" as the Word says, that is, to do it to help someone else.

"None of us are an island" is a phrase my mother used to tell us as we were growing up whenever we siblings tried to wiggle our way out of helping each other or assuming responsibility for each other. She was right then, and she's still right about this. All of us, no matter how much we hate to admit it, are connected to and have a need for someone else. That's the way God designed and intended us. He designed us to need each other. Now, "need" is not meant to be taken in a literal sense, as in you need another person to survive. No, that's not accurate. The only person you will ever need in this life, whose existence be life or death for you and you need them to survive, is Jesus Christ. His existence was life or death for you such that He died so you could live. John 3:16, paraphrased, states God was so gracious and kind toward us that He gave up what meant the most to Him, His Son, so that we could live. That was sacrifice; that was unconditional love.

That's how we are supposed to love. We are supposed to have that same type of unconditional love for other people. The Word of God, in Mark 12:30-31, clearly and plainly expresses to us that the first and greatest command from God for our lives is to love Him. We just talked about how our first purpose is to live for Him and bring Him glory, right? By obeying this command, we prove and demonstrate our love for Him and understanding of our purpose. By living and loving Him *first,* wholeheartedly, we bring glory to Him through our actions, what we say and what we do. The Scripture goes on to reveal to us the second commandment, which is to love your neighbor as yourself. To love your neighbor *like* you love yourself. So, another one of our common purposes, no matter who we are, is to love God first, then to love others like we love ourselves.

If we truly love ourselves, how do we treat ourselves? We should treat ourselves with respect, we should treat ourselves like we matter and we should treat ourselves like a special treasure or rare find. When you truly love yourself, you don't intentionally put yourself in harm's way nor do anything that will not help you. If that is the way we love ourselves, then that is the way we are to love and treat others according to God's standard.

All of us have this common purpose from God, to love others and to help each other. All of us have an obligation to be kind and gracious toward others because God has done so for us. No matter what you do occupation or career-wise, even down to your interests, in living out your purpose, all of it ultimately can and should be somehow beneficial to someone else.

The problem with purpose number two is so many people don't truly love God nor do they love themselves. Or, they don't love God enough while loving themselves too much. If you find yourself in either of these scenarios, chances are you aren't fully living out and living in purpose because to do so, you have to follow the outline given to us in the Word of God. The good news is you don't have to stay this way.

If I could insert an emoji here, I would.

This isn't some death sentence where you have to eat one last Level 5000, disgusting meal and then you are fried. No. As long as there is breath in your body, you still have time to get this right. You want to be a person who lives for God with everything you have and a person of great use in His Kingdom. In order to do that, you first have to really know Him, then you must truly understand that the world is a big place, bigger than you.

We are all in this world to help someone else be better and do better. You truly are your brother's keeper. Just like Cain asked God that one time in the Bible in Genesis chapter four. The story of Cain and Abel is the first crime story in history. (Way before The First 48 was produced, there was the Bible, and the storyline is very suspenseful too, if I may add.)

You see, either way you slice it, Cain wasn't living in and definitely was not living out purpose.

Let's look at it.

Cain was that guy who knew of God, but didn't know God.

Ouch. How can you say such a thing, Adara? Well, if he knew God, he would have been living his life in a way that was satisfying to God instead of worrying over how his brother was living. That's number one. Number two, we said to fulfill purpose is to help and love someone else the way you love yourself. Cain couldn't have possibly loved himself if he could take the life of someone else, let alone his own flesh and blood.

I know you're thinking. Dang, that's really cold.

It *was* cold. It was so cold Cain was not conscious of the fact that as God's creations, we are formed and designed to love Him as well as others. That is His purpose for us. It's been that way from the beginning. From the beginning, God saw it was not profitable for people to be by themselves. He literally said, in Genesis 2:18 NLT, *"It is not good for the man to be alone."* Because God is so awesome, and so in tune with what we really need and what's best for us, He set things in motion for man and tried to find him a helper, a companion. He made the animals first, and when that didn't quite do it, He made a person just like him—another human. That speaks volumes. The help we need is another person, and God knew that. That's why He has created so many of us. We each carry and possess the ability to be the answer for someone else.

If only Cain had clear vision instead of being a hater. God created his parents, two of them, to love each other and be good to each other, but everything got messed up when sin came into the picture.

Sin complicates everything. Cain didn't take the hint. There was more to life than him and his emotions. Neither did he follow the blueprint God laid out. Cain didn't get the hint that Abel wasn't his enemy; they were the same. He didn't understand God had a purpose and a special job for him because he was too busy minding Abel's business. He went ahead and killed his brother.

Insert emoji again, not a good news one.

How many of us are like Cain? We don't know what we were made to do on this earth because we lack knowledge and understanding of the One who made the earth, who made us, and we are too busy minding what other people are doing. We're too busy complaining about how good someone else's life seems instead of focusing on God so we can live the life He intends for us.

Poor little Cain. He was confused and that confusion drove him to a terrible place in his emotions. It all stemmed from the fact that he didn't truly love God nor himself so he couldn't love his brother. Even sadder—well, not truly that sad, but still worthy of mentioning—is that his brother, Abel, *did* follow God's blueprint. Abel did the exact opposite of Cain. Abel was living out both of God's purposes for his life. He was worshipping God and offering up a sacrifice—bringing God glory and honoring Him while also serving and loving his brother. He did not hate on his brother nor envy him or harm him, and we can infer that he loved Cain because Cain is the only person the Bible attests to as having hatred. The Bible never says Abel hated Cain. That means Abel did the opposite of his brother and he loved Cain. He treated him no less than he loved himself. He was able to do this because he first loved God.

Man. Picture that.

It can be done.

From this story, we can take some lessons and surely see how our common purpose is to look out for each other and be good to each other. Some of us get it. We truly are walking with and loving on God, and this translates into and through our interactions with people. Others of us have to learn this as we learn of God, and that is okay. I had to learn how to properly love others because my definition of love was jaded, misplaced and based off self, just like poor little Cain.

When I died to self and stopped believing everything was about me, I began to walk and live under God's standards and my interactions with people subsequently changed. Thank God, I never killed anybody, but I have been the "bad guy" because I didn't understand God's love for me nor did I truly love myself. Once I began to tap into the realization of both God's love and self-love, then started for serious—yes, I said "for serious"—to take God seriously, then loving people correctly and in a healthy manner came so easily and naturally.

Before that I didn't know what love really was. I was so selfish. I wanted so badly to be seen and liked and admired and have all attention on me. I had a self-esteem issue because I was unhappy with the girl I saw staring back at me, and that unhappiness manifested itself in my relationships. That's how I got involved with a boy and lost my virginity so young. That's how I made other poor choices when it came to men. I was looking for the love in them that I didn't see in me.

I never got it.

Not only were they unable to give love to me on the magnitude for which I was so desperate, but the love that one very nice guy tried to show me, I rejected. It wasn't good enough. Like I said, I've been the bad guy. I messed with someone's feelings. I was grimy, but my behavior came back around for me.

After I started to see how wrong I was, it came back so hard, at one point I began to wonder if I would ever fall in true love.

But God showed me that the answer was yes. It was yes then, and it's still yes. He also clearly showed me how the natural law of reaping all that you sow is real. Reaping what you sow is very real. That's why it's beyond important to sow what is of God and what is good so you can receive back to you what is from God and what is good.

I've started to receive back some of my good—after getting real help and healing from God. Back then, in my grimy days, it was epic chaos on the inside for me. It was like a cycle I can only liken to that poor little hamster on the wheel going in a pointless circle. A pointless, endless circle was pretty much what I felt I was doing, and I never got what I was looking for where I was looking. I was looking in the wrong places. I was looking at what was around me.

Like Cain did, I compared myself to others. I was a chronic comparer. I tried to mimic what I saw. I didn't like the way I looked for a long time, and I had trouble with self-esteem. I knew I was "pretty" to some degree because people had told me all my life, but I never felt like it. Guys liked me, but I was never the girl they drooled and fought over. I secretly wanted that. I envied girls who had the juice like that! Like Cain, I was so focused on what those other girls had and did that I wasted precious time out of my life. That envy, that low self-esteem is what moved me to seek attention and validation from the likes of social media and men. I wanted guys to admire me the way they admire video and Insta-vixens, so I tried to imitate what I saw. Other women *seemed* to be winning that way and I wanted to win, too. I'm not too high class now that I'm scared to admit it.

Little by little—literally—I "started wearing less and going out more". (I told you this wasn't going to be your average book.) I made myself extra sexy. Clearly, I was not living out either of our common purposes. Nothing about what I was doing, who I did it with or how I presented myself brought any glory to God. It definitely wasn't indicative of someone who loves herself or even others. It hurt me, hurt my self-esteem further and hurt my family. It was just an all-inclusive, all-round bad news trip.

I'm happy to share with you today—the wonderful person reading my story, whoever you are—that upon finally finding God, all of that changed. I started living for real. I started to change my ways. He began to live through me, and it was then, through that healing process, I learned about individual purpose. I learned of my purpose. I learned the point and purpose of everything that happened to me. As ugly as it got, in time, it all has become that much more beautiful. Truly, God gives us beauty for all of our ashes.

Chapter 5

No, But Really, About This

Purpose Thing...

I guess by now the secret is out. I was pretty unhappy. I came from a good home, got good grades, had family and people who at the time I considered friends. I've been working since age fifteen so I had a little money to myself, and yet I was unhappy. There was this deep inner depression I could not shake, stemming from my poor choices in life. Unhappiness drove me to do some stupid things and make even more poor choices, like taking allergy medicines, then drinking two tall Four Lokos because I wanted to have fun and escape my pain.

I know for a fact God has a divine purpose for and has been watching over my life because this one particular instance I'm about to tell you about—which was my wakeup call—was one of several in which I could have been attacked, raped, beaten or worse. None of that happened. I put myself in some pretty dumb situations and hung out with some less than desirable people. They were not in the right mind and couldn't think for themselves, let alone think for me. It's pretty risky business to place your life in the hands of people who don't value life at all. I've been extremely careless with my life several times...and God watched over me.

I've been careless enough to get into a car with a home girl who was as drunk as a skunk, who then let her boyfriend, who's also drunk, drive. I've been that girl who innocently placed a drink down on a bar top, then turned away long enough for someone to slip something into it. I've been that girl who met someone in the club I didn't know and took them home with me for the night. I did it and nobody had a clue.

But God kept me.

I owe my life to Him because He spared it over and over. I came out of each of these situations unharmed and untouched. Never contracted an incurable disease. Never got into a driving-while-intoxicated accident. Never been drugged. Never ever. Some people have not been as fortunate, so I share my story as a warning for anyone who currently engages in these type of activities. Not only is this behavior not smart, it is not safe. This is not God's best for your life. You can short circuit your life, and that's not what you really and truly want deep, deep down.

I know it's not. It isn't what I wanted, but I kept engaging in risky behavior until one day when everything changed and my eyes came open.

God got my attention using the very thing I was going hard with in rebellion to do it. I got a real, good reality check. I don't even remember all of the events surrounding the night I decided I didn't want to live that way anymore, but I've been able to piece together what happened based on what I've been told, what I remember and what God has brought to my recollection in my dreams.

I remember this particular Saturday night. I went about my shenanigans as usual, getting dressed in my mirror in some skimpy outfit, then going to NYC to meet up with my friends. I remember pre-gaming as usual, having mixed a drink at home, upstairs in my bedroom, to get as much of a buzz as I could so I wouldn't have to spend too much money on drinks inside the spot. I remember taking the Long Island Railroad into the city with that little mixed concoction in a Poland Spring water bottle. I slowly sipped during the whole train ride, and I got my desired buzz. I took my sexy selfie, paired it with some sexually suggestive song lyrics, as usual, then posted it and waited to see how many likes and comments it would get. That was routine for me. That was a normal Saturday night.

I remember arriving in the city and going to the place where I was supposed to meet up with some friends. It was a little bar downtown, nothing too fancy, and the drinks were smooth, but strong, if you were into that sort of thing. You would leave "right," meaning, just the right amount of drunk to go home to your man, woman—whoever you were into—and do whatever you were into. It was the perfect low-key turn up, a low "lituation" if all else flopped and plans fell through.

I was at one of my go-to spots. I had finished my personal potion and wanted to keep the buzz going, so I was about to order a drink. My friends still hadn't arrived and I was at the bar by myself when I ran into a former classmate/associate. He and I were somewhat cool from high school days, although we had not seen each other in a super long time. It was nice to catch up. Well, catching up over shots and mixing dark and light liquors was not exactly smart. You see, I forgot I had started the night out drinking all light liquor. My night started with Svedka. My high school friend and I were taking shots of Hennessey and Jack Daniels at the bar. If you've ever drunk liquor, you know rule number one is *never* mix anything dark with anything light. (There's a whole other message I can preach in that, but I won't... at least not right now.)

I haphazardly mixed dark and light drinks and even had Jack Daniels with coffee or some type of caffeine in it, which, by the way, was the most disgusting thing I've ever tasted in my life. I drank it because I was a little sleepy and needed to wait for my friends to come through. The bartender said it would keep me up. Well, an hour later, the crew was still a no-show. My drinking partner got a call and had to leave. He had asked if I was going to leave too, and I said no.

I was feeling good. Shoot, why would I leave? Everybody had bailed on me, but it was fine. I was used to going out alone to the bar some nights anyway. I told him he could leave and that I was going to stay. He was apprehensive, but I promised I would be okay and told him I wasn't alone.

At that moment, I had no idea the severity or seriousness of what I was saying, but thanks be to God, I truly wasn't alone. I had angels standing over and watching over me and I had grace over my life. This night I would really need them.

My friend left. I stayed...and kept drinking. Continued drinking meant I didn't have to go home and eventually sober up.

Sobering up meant facing the fact I was living a lie and was rebelling against what I knew I was supposed to be doing. Drinking was my escape from guilt and shame. Drinking blocked out everything. I felt happy for however long the buzz lasted. So, I continued to drink and I was fine. I sat there for hours, pacing myself with my drinks. The moment I decided I had had enough and that I would travel back to Long Island by myself was when the real "party" started. On my journey back to Penn Station, on some back street, so drunk from all those drinks and mixing them together, I passed out. God later showed me this was the first of two times I passed out that night.

I woke up somewhere between three and four in the morning on my front steps to my mother in tears and screaming at me and my father carrying me off the front stairs with a look of disappointment and confusion in his eyes. Coming back to consciousness, all I heard was my mother yelling, "I've had enough, Darren. This time she could have been killed. Do you realize how serious this was, Adara? Answer me!" My father was helping me out of my vomit-covered coat and into my bed with my mom stomping behind us still yelling. (That's what moms do when they care. They go on and on and on...)

My bed seemed so far away, but I was overjoyed to see it. It was just what I needed. My head was spinning and I felt very weak. My dad asked my mom to leave the room so he could talk to me. She agreed, then stormed out upset. From the edge of the bed, he very calmly and softly began to speak to me.

I imagine I must have smelled horribly, judging by how far away from me and how close to the door he was. He softly began to tell me they had been awakened by the security alarm on our house blaring loudly when the door was opened without being decoded and the alarm bypassed. They awakened to see me barely conscious, half in the house and half out the front screen door. My key was still in the door. Someone opened the door for me and placed my ID on my coat. He explained that somebody had brought me back from wherever I had been. With tears forming in his eyes, he explained that my mother had heard a serious rustling as the blaring began. My mom saw me lying there in my throw up, reeking of liquor, and she faintly saw whoever had brought me home as they sped away from the house, frightened by the alarm. There was no sign of me being hurt aside from the rip in my jeans at the knees which I looked down and saw for myself.

It was in this moment, with a blaring headache, it started to hit me that I had to get my life together. The look of hurt, confusion, shock, disappointment, and yet thankfulness that I was alive I saw in my father's eyes broke something inside of me. I knew I had been spared.

Of course, I suffered the worst hangover you can imagine. Judging by the way my stomach and face felt, I had thrown up violently many times. I wasn't able to attend church that Sunday. My parents let me stay home to recover.

This was big. My parents had a rule: everyone who lived under their roof had to be in church on Sunday morning. If I could party Saturday night, I could get up for church on Sunday.

Naturally, I was grateful they allowed me to stay home that Sunday to recover, but beyond that, I later found out, they covered my dirty laundry in public. They didn't out me to the congregation or put my business, *our* business, on blast. I slept most of the day, but when I did wake up, I woke to text messages from a few saints checking on me to make sure I was okay. They had heard I wasn't feeling well.

My parents didn't make me a spectacle out of me. They simply told those who asked I was sick. They didn't condone what I had done, but they also didn't pronounce doom and gloom over me or embarrass me. They really and truly put the greater good of holding our family together and remaining unified at the forefront, no matter what chaos was happening behind closed doors. They didn't sweep what happened under the rug or pretend like I didn't do something terrible, but I also wasn't condemned or banned from the family.

That spoke volumes to me. That helped wake me up to the reality that this notion that I wasn't loved, an idea which I'd held on to for so long, was a lie. A bald-faced, dumb lie I had allowed the enemy to spoon feed me day after day, night after night.

That right there—what my parents did for me—was the epitome of love. It wasn't being fake or phony; it was loving and caring and protecting. It was through that experience I began to see my parents in a different light and began to see God in a different light. Through that particular experience, I began to see what true love and grace—Godly love and Godly grace—look like in action.

It was just like that time love covered up Noah's dirty laundry in Genesis chapter nine. Noah had gotten drunk as skunk (sound familiar?) and started acting less than desirably. He got so drunk, he disrobed himself in front of everyone. His children came and covered him. In that place where he was vulnerable and exposed to any and everything, where he wasn't cognizant or coherent, they thought on their feet, covering him and thinking for him. His children acknowledged his actions were out of order and shameful, but they did not leave him there or condemn him. They cleaned him up and covered "the dirty laundry," i.e. the way they found him, an unkempt, drunken hot mess.

That's what my parents did for me, not only in this particular instance, but others as well. They covered me and protected me, or at least they tried to, to the best of their ability.

God began to show me what grace really looked like. Whereas I should have been and rightfully deserved to be exposed as the rebellious, unruly teenage-to-adult terror I had become, my parents kept their peace. I knew for sure they had to love me after this particular event when I didn't get kicked out of the house. Not only had I broken curfew—again—my actions resulted in a stranger having access to our home because that person had had the key and was able to open the door and place me on the stairs.

Later on in a dream, God showed me it was a man around my age who found me and brought me all the way back to Long

Island, unharmed and untouched. Nothing happened to me aside from falling and ripping my jeans. I didn't fall victim to rape or sexual assault. I didn't get beaten, stabbed or dismembered. NOTHING HAPPENED TO ME. Every hair was where it was supposed to be, sort of—it was a mess from my throwing up everywhere and sweating and falling out, but you get my point. That man assumed responsibility for me even though he had no ties to me. (That will preach specifically to the ladies.)

A complete stranger protected me and made sure I made it safely to my home. That was nothing and nobody but God. That was divine protection. That was grace on my life. It was also protection over my family because that person could have intruded into our home and hurt us all. He had access to my ID with our address and my key. I could no longer act blind to or ignore what had happened. I guess you could think of another explanation, but in my heart *I know* God spared my life and had His divine angels over me. He moved that man to bring me home. What other logical explanation is there?

God later showed me that right before I slipped out of consciousness, I asked that man not to tell my parents and not to bother them because I'd already done enough to hurt them and they didn't have to know. It's amazing how guilt consumes us, even subconsciously, and how we chain ourselves to defeat and despair unnecessarily. In my head, I had convinced myself I was just one more wrong move away from being cut off forever. That was dumb on my part because parents know everything and they love you regardless—just like God does.

Who did I really think I was fooling, though? I mean, really? Although I was a good student and got stellar grades and excelled, I had some issues and they were evident in the way I partied so much, drank so much and was mad at the world all the time. I always had an attitude when I was sober and I never wanted to be home unless it was to sleep. That is not normal behavior and it was noticed. Although I did a good job of hiding my pain for a while, guilt and regret eventually consumed me and I began to lash out at everyone because I had no peace. Having no peace and definitely not feeling like I had a purpose or point for existence drove my attitude and behavior. I'm grateful it was noticed and handled the right way.

If you are a parent reading this, I encourage you to pay attention to your children. They will never admit it, but they want your attention no matter how old they are. They want to know you care. Even if your child is well-behaved and a top-performing student or athlete or whatever, they still can and will have their own way of needing you and reaching out for you. At some point, no matter how "grown" they assert themselves to be, a child will need a parent to nurture and nurse them back to health, whether in the literal, physical sense or in terms of coping and navigating through tough situations.

I thought my parents were against me after the things I had done. In actuality, they drew that much closer to me. They were aware something was really wrong. They wanted me to be better. They wanted to help me fix what was wrong, and so they prayed and fasted and gave me the space I needed to work through my internal issues. The whole time I thought I was fighting alone and kept secrets to protect them, they knew through the Spirit everything that was happening. They did what they knew best—prayed and let God work. Eventually, I finally got it through my head that I wasn't alone. Had I just been honest and opened up about my struggles, things could have gone differently and I could have saved myself a lot of hurt, pain and mistakes.

Unbeknownst to me, God had been showing my mom visions of everything I was doing wrong. She had dreams and literally felt things when it came to me. No matter how much I lied to her, she was able to call out specifics of everything I had done. I denied and lied so much, but she knew. She never pushed and pried or did any type of deep investigation, but oh boy, did she find out everything because God revealed things to her I wasn't strong enough to say. Although the events of that particular night took my parents by surprise because they had no clue where I was or who I was with, they knew I was in trouble and they already were praying and interceding on my behalf.

Nothing I do takes my folks by surprise which truthfully scares me a little bit, especially when it comes to my mom. Mothers just know things. Well, I don't know about yours, but mine does. If I'm not feeling well, she can look at me and pinpoint what's wrong. Isn't that a reflection of God? Nothing we do takes God by surprise and even in the midst of our wrong, He loves us and offers us another chance.

In the midst of doing wrong, we know what's right. That's how Adam and Eve immediately knew they were naked and were shamed. God designed us that way, yet we blatantly choose wrong. Even subconsciously, I knew I was called to a higher standard than what I was doing. That night was such a wake-up call for me. It was time to get myself together and stop running. Running was tiring...and dangerous. Running was hurting me and the people I loved. I never meant to drag my family into my mess. It was time to get out of this and time to find out what exactly and specifically God wanted with a girl like me.

Why had He kept *me* alive?

It became crystal clear to me God spared my life for a purpose I could not escape. God preserved my life because He wanted me to tell others about this experience—about all my experiences—and turn hearts back to Him. I didn't see back then, but God had a purpose and plan for all of my pain. Although my true deliverance did not fully and completely happen right there in that moment, it was in that setting I knew I could no longer blatantly run from God. I understood the next time I did something careless of this magnitude, I would not be so fortunate. Although grace is sufficient, it is not to be recklessly abused or misused. The seed of heartfelt repentance took root and started to grow right from that eye-opening experience.

This was my warning to stop playing and surrender now or pay a much graver cost, one I couldn't afford to pay, later. It was time to say yes to the purpose God had for me.

I was not oblivious to that purpose, no matter how much I tried to play dumb or ignore it. I knew in my heart ministry was my purpose. I knew I was called to preach. As I previously said, though, not only was it not what I wanted, I was afraid of this purpose and felt like I wasn't good enough or qualified. I questioned how I could speak to people about the Lord when I hadn't followed Him the way I was supposed to all my life. I had made horrible decisions. I hoped and prayed God would stop tugging at my heart, stop calling me and just let me be.

It never happened. He never stopped pulling and tugging and in fact, the call intensified until I gave in. Someone has to surrender, God or us. Who do you think it will be?

Right. It has to be us.

I had these vivid, clear, reoccurring dreams about me preaching to crowds and doing conferences. I saw myself in front of mass audiences. I remember waking up in a cold sweat at the thought of preaching and public speaking, completely petrified at the mere thought of that being even close to reality because I didn't think I was good enough in terms of capability or character. The last thing I wanted was to make myself a bigger hypocrite than I already had been by getting up on Sundays like everything was all good, knowing I had had sex the night before or was struggling through a hangover from the way I got sloppy drunk the night before.

I can remember crying out many nights, asking God like, "Yo, what do You want with me? Can't you choose somebody else?"

He started talking back to me, like "Yes, I could choose somebody else, but I didn't because I wanted and still want *you*." He clearly told me He was going to use every bad, reckless, careless, selfish choice I had ever made. He was going to turn them into something good so He could be seen and give someone hope. He began to show me my desire to be a teacher would manifest and come true, just not in the traditional classroom setting I had planned.

Oh yeah, we had several conversations about this change of plans and I fought Him on that, too. I was content with just getting my degrees and being a great teacher to kids because I love children. However, God had much more for me than that and He very plainly told me so. God showed me His true purpose for me was to minister to and teach others about Him through candid, raw, uncut truth about all my life encounters. This would require much boldness, tough skin, humility, sometimes harsh backlash, but ultimately, it would set me free.

Although salvation sets us free and whoever is in Christ is free, we also are overcome by the words of our testimony. True freedom comes from the ability to share what you've survived to help someone else survive.

I'm living freely now because I'm able to write and speak freely about the past without shame and offer someone else hope and encouragement. The strength I have isn't mine to claim. It's not of my doing. It comes from surrendering to God and deciding to live in and live out His purpose for me.

I've embraced the entire process. It's been a long process. I didn't just wake up and become a better person. I had to be purged and cleaned up and made a new. Jesus did that for me. You would never know by looking at me now how broken I truly was. I'm thankful for everything I went through because I am learning more and more that I'm not the only person who has gone through something like this. I know God let me survive in order to help others survive. I'm living out my purpose by telling the world what the Lord has done for me and trying to win hearts for Him, but also by trying to build others up so they never have to be as broken as I was.

Chapter 6

There's a Purpose for Me...

But What Else?!?

It's kind of like I'm a volunteer firefighter. I'm not being paid top notch money to risk it all every day and do what I do, but I am needed. Somebody somewhere needs me to be alert and answer the call for help. Somebody somewhere needs me to be bold and brave and dive into the fire where they are and help them get out because they can't get out themselves. I would want someone to help me if I were in danger and they had the answer. I have the answer and His name is Jesus, and so I volunteer to fight the spiritual fire for people and help bring them out safely from the flames of the enemy's territory.

My plan was to teach high school Global and American History and retire somewhere tropical and secluded when I was old. God's plan, however, is to mold and make me into a spiritual volunteer firefighter. While I am still teaching, while I still love history, I've fully walked into what is required of me without fear because my life is bigger than me.

We're still talking about purpose. In purpose, our lives are bigger than us. My individual purpose is so evident I never again can front and fake like I don't know what it is. The purpose for my pain has begun to unfold and blossom in a way I never expected. I wouldn't have believed it if someone told me back then that one day I would be writing and telling people how premarital sex, abortion, failed relationships, poor self-esteem and falling prey to the trap of social media as a means to validation and self-worth were bad things that happened in my life, but were a part of God's purpose and will for my life so He, with His saving, healing power, would be seen and revealed to me and to others.

It's interesting and kind of funny to me that the very things I did and used and abused before are the things most critical and essential to what I do now, but that's really how it goes. What the enemy uses against us, God will use to empower and groom us for what He wants to do through us. I was that girl who looked to social media as a means to be noticed. Now that I've surrendered to God, I get noticed all day every day. Notifications boom all day every day. My social media no longer belongs to me, in a sense. Isn't that crazy? I wanted those 'likes' so badly. I wanted to be someone well known, respected and valued by people. Now, from serving God and being obedient, that notoriety has come to me on a level that's overwhelming at times because so many people have access to my page. The desire to be liked was not wrong; I just expressed it wrongly. But now, the very same thing I desired for the wrong reasons, God has turned into something right. Whatever you search for, you can have—if you go through and go to God to get it.

You're probably thinking there's no way God could take your worst pain and turn it around for something good, that there's no way you in turn might be able help someone else, but the truth is He can. Each and everything we've gone through and everything we will go through has an intended point. Every aspect of your life is a part of the overall puzzle, and every single piece matters.

A puzzle is not complete without every piece. Your life will not unfold the way it's supposed to unless everything happens the way it's supposed to. Of course, we put ourselves in some situations, and there are things that happen to us that are way beyond the scope of our control. The good news is that even those things beyond our control, God has under control. If you take nothing else away from my story, I hope it's crystal clear that God loves you and He can use you no matter what you have done or what mistakes you have made. If He found room for an off-the-wall girl like me, therein lies proof anybody and everybody is an eligible candidate for His purpose and for His glory. The key is to acknowledge this life is to be lived through Him and with Him, and then let God guide you.

Being a school teacher set the tone and precedent for my becoming a preacher and has greatly helped me because the two roles are extremely similar. Teachers have to read the materials through and through for understanding for themselves, then communicate the information to others who may or may not be familiar with it. Teachers spend hours preparing materials, handouts and hands-on visual aids. Teaching is not the highest paid occupation and often times much of your personal life revolves around it, but like the infamous saying goes, when you do what you love, you never work a day in your life.

How is being in ministry like being a school teacher? As a minister, or a person who preaches the Gospel, you spend hours reading the Word of God, trying to master and perfect what is inside of it. You have to communicate the teachings to others based on what is inside you along with the inspiration of the Holy Spirit. A good minister or preacher, one who takes ministry very seriously, spends hours perfecting the sermons he or she delivers. As with being a school teacher, sometimes the ministerial profession is not regarded and respected, and sometimes preachers are not compensated the way they should be monetarily or with recognition. Preaching and ministry are two things I say nobody in their right mind volunteers to do because they require so much of oneself. I did not volunteer. I kicked and screamed, figuratively speaking. I barked at people. I wasn't about to turn into something I didn't want to be. I was going to "do me." I had no intentions of being in ministry.

In my head, my pastor parents had no life and never had time for themselves. I was not having that. I saw the way they always had somewhere to go and something to do—how someone always needed help—and I assumed they had no time to do the things that interested them. I didn't understand with great sacrifice comes great reward, and there were great rewards. All I saw was the responsibility and how much sacrifice came with it.

Doing work as if directly for God has many perks. I went to undergraduate school for free because of my parent's obedience to God. I got a full four-year academic scholarship to SUNY Old Westbury because my dad was ministering in the right place at the right time. It didn't click for me back then, but I see now how much favor that was. God has been behind the scenes working out every single detail of my life, even when I wasn't concerned about my life. I was not even entertaining the thought of ministry. As far as I was concerned, ministry was boring and I couldn't have fun. But the more I fought and ran from it, the louder and stronger the feeling that I was supposed to be doing ministry became. You can run, but you cannot hide, and you definitely cannot outrun God. I tried...and failed miserably.

The first time I dreamed I was preaching, I woke up in a cold sweat, my bangs sticking to my forehead. I was hyperventilating and fighting to regain my composure. It was so vivid and so clear. In fact, my trial sermon happened exactly as I saw it in my dreams. That was scary at the time because I didn't see how it was possible. A time was coming and coming soon wherein I had to choose God or chase after the lifestyle I was trying to create. I would have to make some serious choices, including letting people go who I loved. God speaks in various ways, including visions and dreams. He clearly spoke, beckoning and calling out to me even while I slept. To this day, He deals with me in my dreams, but the dreams about preaching got my attention. I ignored them, but they kept recurring until I couldn't ignore them anymore. I couldn't shake them no matter how hard I tried.

I thought the dreams would stop, but they didn't. I called myself ignoring His call and sending Him to voicemail, forgetting He has multiple ways of getting in contact with people. He didn't only speak to me in dreams. People I knew as well as strangers called it right out—you're going to be a preacher. You cannot ignore purpose. You have a choice whether to fulfill it, but you cannot ignore it, just like you cannot ignore or deny your existence.

Like it or not, no matter what is currently going on in your life, you are alive. That's enough proof that God wants to use you. The only people who cannot be used by God are those currently in the grave. You aren't, and thus, He can use you, but you have to make the choice to let Him. You have to want to walk in His purpose for you. I only had complete rest after I began to do what I was born and created to do. There is a certain level of satisfaction in life that only comes from living out your purpose and doing what God has said.

Perhaps you do not know your individual purpose yet. Don't panic. Don't hyperventilate, and please kindly don't chuck this book. This isn't designed to condemn you or make you nervous. At minimum, it's my prayer and hope you start to question your purpose and go looking to God for the answer. I didn't wake up knowing mine either. Please never think that. Although I had those dreams and that gut feeling, God had to reveal His plan to me and show my purpose to me. I had to ask Him, "What exactly do You want from me, God?", then wait for the answer.

The first step toward finding purpose is finding God. If you have not found Him yet, the good news is you're alive and you still have time. The second step is building a relationship with Him through prayer and reading His Word, i.e. the Bible.

Prayer, in the simplest of explanations, is a conversation. In a conversation, there is dialogue. You speak and you are spoken to. Talk to God, confide in Him the way you would a friend, but also let Him talk back to you. Ask Him questions, by all means, but be patient and wait for Him to respond.

God's voice will be distinct; you will know it's Him. It will bring you peace. While it won't sound like Darth Vader—like I thought it would when I first got saved—it can be audible, but definitely not fiction-like or funny sounding.

God speaks through His written Word as well. Pick up your Bible. Open the app on your phone and read and let the words of God comfort and speak to you. Let God reveal your individual purpose in addition to bringing glory to Him and living a life that reflects Him living inside of you. Ask God to show you how your experiences, good or bad, directly connect to your destiny. Let Him show you how the things at which you are naturally good and gifted could and should be used for His purpose and in His kingdom. Above all, pray for direction. Ask Him to point you in the right direction so you won't be lost or confused.

This is a prayer you can pray regarding purpose:

Lord, I ask you today to begin to uncover the individual purpose or purposes You have for me. It's my desire to live a fulfilled life and do things that are meaningful, but I know that cannot happen without You and Your guidance. I ask that You begin to expose to me what You expect and require of me. I ask that as I consistently pray this prayer and read Your Holy Word that You would speak to me and bring clarity about the course of my life. I know my steps are ordered and planned by You, so I will trust and be guided by

You. I want to live a life that is pleasing to and honors You. I want to be a powerful, sharp, useful tool in Your kingdom. So I ask in prayer that You begin to work in me and on me, and show me my purpose.

In Jesus' name, I pray,

Amen.

The concept of prayer is not hard. Continue to pray and ask God to reveal to you what He wants from you. Be consistent with your prayer regarding this. Let God show you and be on the lookout for the ways He will confirm it for you. God will never speak and not send some sort of confirmation or otherwise bring you clarity. He will also give you the means and the wherewithal to make everything happen. Keep at it with Him and let Him uncover His purpose for your life.

Perhaps you already know your purpose, know exactly what you're supposed to be doing. Great! I'm glad you do. My question is what steps are you taking on your end to make your purpose happen? Perhaps you need a little encouragement—a gentle push from a sister in Christ and a friend. I would like, if I may challenge you, to ask you to remember that moment when you first realized what you were born to do. Remember how liberated and free you felt? Remember how excited and passionate you were? You couldn't wait to get started or take the world by storm. I want you to remember that time and that place and ask God to ignite that fire again. Get that burning back on the inside of you, to the point you start pursuing whatever it is God told you to do.

Someone out there needs your purpose from you. God needs your purpose from *you*. He equipped you to do whatever He has asked you to do. So today, right now, I pray you get the strength to chase after your purpose with everything you've got. I'm doing it, too. It's never going to be easy, and I would never lie and tell you it will be, but I can tell you it will be so worth it. Level-5000 worth it. So go on and do it. I know you can.

Love, *Adara*

Chapter 7

Finding My Piece of Peace

My favorite story in the entire New Testament of the Bible hands down is the story of the prodigal son in Luke 15:11-31. It's a short, but powerful story about true love. Not true love in the romantic sense—it's not a novella or a Harlequin book—but it is a story about love. It's the story of how a kid left home to find his way. The kid came from a good home, he had a sibling and his father was very wealthy. One day, this kid has the ingenious idea that, because he is grown, he is entitled to live life on his own terms—you know, "doing him."

So, this kid demands his share of his father's money, what he would get when his father died. That's super messed up and kind of bold to say to your parent, "Hey, give me my part of your estate even though you're not dead." That's essentially what happened. The boy asks for his share of all the money and the estate, and the father agrees. So, the boy moves out to live on his own and be "grown." Well, everything is all fun and games until he goes bankrupt. Everything is cool until he loses everything. He foolishly spends his entire share of the money on parties and turning up until absolutely nothing is left.

The Bible relays to us that a famine hits the land. Because he has no more money, he begins to starve. In order to survive, he has to take the only job he can find and convinces a farmer to let him work. The farmer agrees and sends him to look after and feed the pigs. Prior to this farmer, no one is willing to help him or feed him. Starvation is so real for him at this point that the slop and mud he is giving to the pigs looks tasty. He has nothing.

The young man comes to his senses. He recalls how he came from a wealthy family and how his father's employees eat and live well. Thus, how shameful and unnecessary is it that he is slowly dying of hunger? He begins to think and takes the first step to recovery by admitting he has been wrong. He repents and convinces himself to go home. Home is where his heart is; home is where love is. There is even food. The son knows everything he has ever really needed is at home, and it is up to him to get back there.

He decides to humble himself and head home. His plan is to ask for his father's forgiveness and ask his father to make him a servant in his house. It feels like he has forfeited the chance to be called "son." So, the young man starts his journey home. While he still is kind of far off in the distance, his father sees him and runs out to meet him. Filled with love for his son, his father hugs him and kisses him.

The young man tells his father he is sorry and that he has sinned against God and him. All he wants now is the chance to be one of his servants, but, the father still treats his son as his son who he loves. He instructs his servants to get his son cleaned up and dressed up so there can be a celebration. The young man is alive, well and has found his way home. The party is live with music and dancing, and while every person at the party isn't happy there is a party, the most important person is very happy: his father.

His father explains why he is so happy and has thrown the party for his son. Before, his son was as though he were dead, lifeless because he was entangled in the wrong things and spiritually dead, but once he came to his senses, now he is revived and has new life and has found his way back home. The son, who was once a prodigal, is redeemed.

This is my story, hence the title, *A Prodigal Princess*. I was the child in this story. I did to my parents what that boy did to his father. They raised me in the Christian faith and provided me with the best of what I needed and wanted, and selfishly, it wasn't enough. Like the prodigal son, when I became of age, I decided that it was time to "do me." I was "grown." I was going to be in charge of myself. Their advice and parenting was no longer useful. I didn't need them.

Rebel was my middle name. I wanted to experience life on my own terms and I thought outside of church was where I would find peace and feelings of completeness and wholeness. My quest for that led me to the highs of marijuana and the lows of club dance floors. Although I never stripped, the strip club was one of my favorite stops on my quest to find myself, along with raves, smoking cyphs, and of course, lounges, clubs, house parties, dorm parties and frat parties. If there was a party, there also was me. From as close as down the block to the bar by where I live in Long Island to as far away as Maryland, even if just for one night, I traveled so I could attend whatever event was happening.

I was searching for peace and something, anything, to make me feel good. It never came from those places. Typically, afterward I would feel worse off than before I went.

Similar to that prodigal son, I wasted money. How I afforded the Gucci Mane "rock star lifestyle, might don't make it" still baffles me because I wasn't flossing in "commas". I had to work hard at the jobs I had. I wasn't rich and truthfully, I couldn't afford the life I was living. Every time I went out, I had a new outfit, fresh hair and of course, a little personalized something to sip on or pull on. Marijuana is not cheap and neither is alcohol. All of this added up: the event tickets, the transportation, my outfits and hair, drinks and so on... I easily squandered thousands of dollars, money that could have been invested or used to make more money.

In the literal as well as the spiritual sense, just like in this story, I was broke. I wasted my resources, then wasted my parents' resources too until everything ran out. I hit rock bottom. I felt empty. I had no peace.

I reached a point where the partying no longer was fun for me. That lifestyle started to drain me. I was going through the motions because it had become so routine for me. Ironically, that same thing happened for me in the church. I was drained and tired from faking the spiritual funk. I just wanted inner peace. Rest. To breathe. To like the person I saw staring back at me in the mirror and to know beyond a shadow of a doubt she was important, no matter what mistakes she made or what happened to her.

I try to explain to people what I was feeling by telling them this period of my life was like catching a Charley horse in the leg, that thing that will stop you dead in your tracks. That's how painful my life was. All you want to do, all you can do is just lay there and take it until it goes away. If you try to stand up before it's completely subsided, you will fall right back down. I inflicted emotional pain on myself through bad choice after bad choice, godless choice after godless choice. Like the prodigal son, I chose my path and decided what I wanted to happen in my life...until it all came tumbling down.

Rock bottom was hard. Breaking acquired bad habits was hard. Losing my self-respect and using sexy pictures to vie for the attention of strangers was hard. Just like how the young man eventually thought feeding and living with the pigs was the best there was for him, I thought surely I wasn't fit for anything good because I'd made mistakes and placed myself in less than honorable situations. Lies the enemy fed me drove me further and further away from the peace and inner stability and security I so desperately wanted and needed.

Deep down, I knew I was better than all of that, but I settled for it because in my mind, I was so far gone, past the point of no return. I psyched myself into thinking my parents despised me, that they didn't love me, only tolerated me and that I had to figure things out all on my own. My own pride was my biggest pitfall because I was so stubborn. Even in the midst of needing real help, I refused to ask for it. I would figure it out.

I too came to my senses. I decided to go back to the place where I knew I would be safe, the safety of God. I had tried everything and everybody else so it was time for me to humble myself and ditch my pride and repent. Rock bottom was the lowest I could go; it couldn't get worse. I had several conversations with myself, fighting my conscience and the need to humble myself and repent. I tried to convince myself I really didn't need anybody and could stop drinking and smoking at any time. If I simply cut out the partying, drinking and smoking, everything would instantly get better. That was false. As I'll explain in the next chapter, I cut all that "bad" stuff out...and I *still* didn't have peace.

Peace didn't come to me until I truly humbled my heart and mind and got honest with myself about everything. The truth hurt, but acceptance of my truth is what started my healing. While I never will advocate for you to beat yourself up or over the head for anything you've done or anything that has happened, I do advocate taking responsibility and ownership for your actions. When I got honest with myself and stopped living in denial, acknowledging I had some serious internal issues, that's when things started to change for the better. Repenting to God and really getting honest with Him was how I began to get up after having fallen so far down. It wasn't until I openly and candidly started to pray, telling God everything—my feelings, my regrets, my fears, what I did and why I did it—it wasn't until then that the burden I carried started to be lifted, little by little. There is a freedom in accepting how things are, even when they're not what you want them to be. That's maturity. Maturity brings a level of freedom and that's how we grow.

Hitting that rock bottom place led me to see there was no place to go but up. I had nothing else to lose and everything to gain from finally stopping all my running, forgiving myself and also forgiving the people who hurt me the most. I forgave, but I also needed to get forgiveness from people. At this point in my life, I still resided under my parents' roof. When I "came home," my waywardness started to decrease. I no longer was blatantly disrespectful or lashed out. No longer did I pick fights in the house, hoping to find an outlet for my emotions. I was undergoing open heart surgery and ironically, it started in a church service, in a revival. I got saved—like *for real* saved—in June 2013.

Chapter 8

Who Do You Love?

Are You for Sure?

My oldest and truest friend since the 5th grade has been Imani Z. Anglin. Back then, she was Imani Z. Bryant, but she's married now. She will kill me if she reads this and I've revealed what the Z in her name stands for. I currently like my life so I won't, but she's my best friend. We met in the fifth grade when life was so simple. My hair was down to mid-waist and I wore it in two long ponytails. I had braces and she wore thick sweaters. We clicked. We instantly bonded tighter than a freshly sewn-in weave because we were so similar, like peas in a pod.

Imani was not a pastor's daughter like me, but she had grown up in church all her life and understood things about me most of the other girls didn't. She understood when my mom didn't let me spend the night or go to the birthday parties because she wasn't allowed to go either. We were, and still are, like ketchup and honey mustard, even though she married and moved to another state. For the past thirteen years, we have been inseparable. Where there's one of us, the other is in very close proximity.

So, back then, we were always together, cutting up and doing crazy things together. Whatever it was, it was usually my bright idea and, after some convincing and because she's my biggest support and my right hand, Imani would be down. One time we decided to run a revival on the playground of our school to save the souls of all the sixth graders who were lost.

Do you believe me yet when I say I had a peculiar childhood?

"Mani", or "Izzy" as I affectionately call her—depending on our mood or the context in which I am speaking and who I'm speaking to—has been more than a blessing to my life. She's changed my definition of what a real gem and real treasure is and embodied the essence of a friend sticking closer than a brother. She and I were different yet similar in so many ways. Little did we know down the line God would use her to be so instrumental in my head-on collision with Him. While we were playing church and playing revival on that playground in 2003, neither of us would have guessed that ten years later we would be in a real revival at the church she attended at the time or that I would be saved during that service. God's hands on and in my life have included my friendships.

Not so much though when it comes to men.

I've had some interesting choices of boyfriends and guys I've taken a liking to. A guy's physical attributes were never solely it for me. I always was attracted to more. Naturally, as a sort of sheltered preacher's daughter, I was attracted to the outgoing, bad boy type. I liked boys who were not afraid of a challenge— bold and thrill-seeking like me. Sadly, I often was less a challenge and more a conquest to them.

Imani was the complete opposite, a very quiet and soft spoken girl. Still is. To this day, it's usually me jumping all around, but I guess that is the beauty of our friendship. We balance each other. She's taught me how to find my seat sometimes and I've taught her how to break out of her shell sometimes. The biggest blessing of our friendship has been her example of a true ride-or-die friend. A true ride-or-die has your best interest at heart even when you don't like the truth and when you are too wrapped up in trouble to see it. A true ride-or-die friend will not stand by and watch you ruin your life. She will not be okay with the bad choices you make—if she really loves you. I've never had to question my best friend or wonder if she was loyal to and loved me. She has proved and solidified this for me over the years through every situation and all the changes I've gone through.

Izzy never liked my choices in the men of my past and made it very clear she didn't care for them. She's had that Level 5000 discernment since we were little kids. So it was no surprise when I broke down and told her I was pregnant. I was panicked and frightened, but I knew she was the one person I could tell and trust. I explained everything to her and how I felt I had only one choice. This was the one time in almost thirteen years of friendship we had a "falling out." I expected her to understand my decision not to keep the baby and be there for me.

I couldn't see it back then, but just because someone isn't cheering on your every move doesn't mean he or she isn't a friend. Real friends with real conscience don't allow other friends to make poor choices. Mani was rightfully disappointed in and hurt by my choices. I knew better; we both did.

While she never rat me out to my parents, it burdened her to watch me go through that process, opening the portal to emotional trauma. Although she supported me emotionally and remained my friend, we drifted apart for a season. Our talks became shorter and shorter and for a brief time we stopped talking all together. I started to use things and people as a coping mechanism and acquired some other friends. She watched me befriend others who would prove to be no good for me. Still, she covered me, called and texted from time to time even though our lifestyles had become way different. I was into the party scene and the fast life; Izzy stuck to what we grew up knowing was right and godly.

One summer night in June of 2013 when we were both on break from our separate colleges, Izzy hit me up to see how I was. We followed each other on social media so I'm more than sure she knew how I was doing. I'm sure she could tell I wasn't taking the breakup I was going through too well. With me, it was lots of clubbing, drinking and seductive, sexy pictures on social media, trying to replace the attention I no longer had from my relationship with the attention of complete strangers. I was jumping from event to event and from guy to guy. I didn't have sexual encounters with each of the guys I talked to or met, but I liked their attention, liked knowing I was attractive to them. The problem was I was not drawing attention in the right way so they weren't attracted to me for the real me.

Social validation was a certain kind of high and when the feeling wore off with one guy, I moved to another. I got bored and simply cut them off. This was a nasty seed I sowed from which I later would reap.

But this particular warm, summer night, Mani invited me to church. The church she attended was having a revival. So, she called me up.

"Hey best, what you are up to tonight?"

Just so happens my plans to go to a party in another state had flopped. The transportation didn't work out and the tickets had sold out. When my best friend who I hadn't seen in a while reached out to me, I was happy to hear from her and eager to see her. I expected her to say, "Let's get up for food and girl time. We can go to Red Lobster, TGI Fridays, or Applebee's" like we had in the past, but to my surprise, the invitation was to hang out at a revival at her church.

You already know I had 5,000 excuses...well, lies...as to why I couldn't go. I had nothing church-appropriate to wear. I had no way there. I was tired. I had to work the next day. I had things to do.

No wasn't an option. Like the little firecracker she is, she had a solution for every excuse I came up with. She picked out the long, blue maxi dress and the denim jacket I would wear. She was my designated ride there and back, and she knew I didn't have to be at work until the afternoon the following day. I had no other reasons I could not go to church with my best friend. I really wasn't fighting or giving excuses to her; I was fighting and giving excuses to God. Just like in the prodigal son story, I had convinced myself I wasn't worthy of forgiveness so why would I have anything to do with church?

I wanted nothing to do with the church because I didn't want to be like those in the church who had hurt me. I didn't want to be a hypocrite. I didn't want to be the person with her hands raised, praising God, knowing I was living foul. For the time being, it was best I didn't go altogether.

This pattern of thinking was all wrong. In fact, thinking like this was the very reason I needed to be in church. Hospitals aren't for healthy people; they are for the sick and hurting. I was hurting and in need of spiritual urgent care. The kind of healing I needed would only come from being inside the house of the Lord and in His presence.

My best friend convinced me to go with her. God used her to tug at my heartstrings because I was fresh out of excuses.

It was in that revival that I got saved.

The speaker's message that night was specifically intended for me—from God for me. There was no way the out of town speaker could have known everything I was battling internally. He spoke directly to everything I was feeling. He talked about running until you are too tired to run, and all you can do is crawl in the other direction. He talked about being disappointed and rejected to the point of questioning God's existence and His love for you. He also talked about guilt from wrong choices and how that guilt forces us to try to things to cope and pacify ourselves when all we have to do is release it to God and let Him repair us.

The preacher touched every single point I was dealing with, and all I could do was sit there and cry. With tears streaming down my face, I began to think, "So what are you going to do, Adara? What's it going to be?" I couldn't keep going in this circle.

I was trapped.

I was trapped in a world of reckless living, casual sex, off and on relationships not going anywhere, drunkenness and searching for validation from people who could never give it to me. If I kept living that way, it eventually would kill me—or I would kill myself. I took too many chances and I was running on low. I could feel the margin for error getting smaller and smaller. God was tapping on my shoulder, asking me if I was done doing me and hurting me. Was I ready now to trust Him?

As I said, that preacher didn't know me and I didn't know him, but it was not a coincidence that that night occurred. That night solidified for me that it was time to come back. It was time to be restored as a princess, no longer running reckless as a prodigal. The sermon closed, the altar was opened up for prayer, but I struggled with going up there. I was self-conscious. I was sure someone in that church knew me and knew my daddy because again, somebody knows him everywhere I go. People had already talked and whispered based on what they saw on social media. I didn't want to go through that any further so I contemplated not going up there. It was going to be a walk of shame and all eyes were going to be on me.

Seeds of fear. Those little seeds of fear were from the enemy. The enemy wanted to keep me trapped from walking up to and into my freedom. Again I say my best friend has a connection to God on another level. She sensed how fearful I was and she nudged me and whispered to me. She said, "Best friend, if you want to go, just go. Nobody is going to look at you, so just go." That was the gentle yet firm push I needed to take that bold step back toward God.

I went. I got out of that pew and walked down to the altar. I wasn't alone; there were others there, too. That was the night I accepted Jesus into my heart. For me. Not for Dad and Mom or for the sake of the church, but for me. I finally did it for me, and it was the best choice I ever made.

After praying the prayer of repentance, I felt this burden and weight begin to be lifted. It was like that relieved feeling you feel when you take a heavy book bag off your back. That's a day I will never forget. I know it was all part of God's plan for my life and I'm thankful for it.

After the service on the way to drop me home, Izzy said my face was different. My color had changed and I had a glow. It wasn't bronzer because I didn't wear too much that night. I can honestly say I started to feel different. There was a stillness and a quietness on the inside. My thoughts weren't racing and the permanent migraine I'd had for so long was lifted. The night I got saved felt like that moment when a wound starts healing properly after you've ripped off the band aid you kept on it for too long. Although the ripping off hurts at first, the pain subsides and, with fresh air, the wound starts to heal. I received Fresh Air for my wounds.

I got honest with myself, asked for forgiveness and invited Jesus into my heart. That's what salvation and repentance is, a turnaround and change of heart. It happened for me that night, all because of an invitation to church. My best friend taught me through that experience that friends let friends have the chance to get to know Jesus. Friends don't let friends walk around blind to or in fear of truth. Friends speak the truth in love and are honest with you. Later on, I really saw how all along Imani had only wanted what was best for me and her honesty was reflective of that. The only person who wasn't honest in this whole situation, who needed to be the most honest, was me. I needed to be honest with myself and others, because the truth was what eventually would set me free.

After I got honest with myself, repented and gave myself back to God, it was time to make things right with my parents. They didn't know the full extent of everything I had done or why, and I knew I wouldn't be free until I told them everything. So I did.

One night shortly after that revival, I broke down and started from the beginning. I asked them just to let me talk and say what I had to say. I apologized for all my wild, obnoxious behavior and of course, in retelling everything, I cried. I told them my story in stages—as I was ready—but the biggest confession and repentance I had to make was about my baby. That was a burden and the source of so much pain I could no longer carry. That choice was the core of all the emotional trauma and why everything spiraled out of control.

Much to my surprise, my parents told me they saw how my perceptions of ministry, church and even them drove me to make that choice. I needed that. Their words broke a yoke for me. They helped me heal by telling me that. While they let me know very clearly they didn't support what I had done, it also was clear they didn't condemn me. Although they made it clear they were disappointed in my choice and how I snuck around and lied and even went so far as to put myself in danger, they also made it very clear they still loved me and I could have come to them for help. At seventeen, I shouldn't have had to worry or even think I had to worry about our family suffering because I was pregnant out of wedlock or worry about how that was going to affect the church Daddy was pastoring.

I needed to know that mistake was forgivable. It would never be excusable, but I wasn't looking to be excused. I was looking for their unconditional love and forgiveness, and I found it. I found forgiveness with God and also with my parents. They had it for me all along, but I couldn't see it.

I learned through this experience that a parent's love is unconditional—through the good and the bad. I came clean about my drinking and substance problems. They already knew about that, but I needed their help in breaking those habits. They asked hard questions about my sexuality and I answered. In those moments, healing started not just for me, but for all of us. We established an open communication that parents and children need with each other.

Healing for me came because my parents didn't throw me out or shun me; instead, they embraced me, took me back and helped me get myself together, just like the prodigal son's father did for him. They saw me taking steps to come back and they met me halfway. The Bible tells that when the prodigal son came to his senses and started to make his way back home, while he was still far out, his father saw him and ran to meet him. That was me. While I still had much work to do and I was still a long ways off from where I needed to be, my parents saw me coming back and met me where I was.

That's exactly how God is too. While you're taking steps toward coming back to the real you, He's moving and leaning in your direction, but you have to turn and go back home. You have to humble yourself and go home. That's what I did.

My parents already knew I was in trouble and waited patiently for me to realize it and make the steps toward recovery I needed. I had to come to the realization that I was in dire need of help. Then, they were there every step of the way and they covered me. While it was clear what they didn't approve of, they respected me as an adult and never played upon the fact that they were my parents. I was a capable adult in their eyes and they allowed me space to grow from everything that happened.

I know they were praying hard. They had to have strong faith because I was definitely defiant and wayward and all that didn't change overnight. I vividly remember walking in past curfew because I simply didn't care, because I was angry at them and the rest of the world and ready to take that anger out on any and everybody. They had to have looked at me and shook their heads sometimes because, quite frankly, I was a knucklehead. Although I've never been arrested or in trouble with the law—by the grace of God—I could have been because majority of my leisure time was spent being belligerent and reckless in my actions, speech and behavior. After we finally had that talk and I came clean, all that bad behavior took on an expiration date. It was like being freed from a prison I'd been locked in for years.

I slowly finally started to change my ways and the inner surgery and healing began for me. It would be a long process. I would make mistakes and slip up, but I had done the hardest part. I got back to attending church—sometimes—and reading my Bible...sometimes. After getting saved, I didn't do a complete life change and everything became perfect. No, salvation was only the beginning, but it is a very significant point in my life and I wanted to be sure I shared my experience in this book.

After repenting and accepting God back into myself—again— and after "coming home" and finally coming clean about everything, something still was not right. Something was still holding me back from fully giving God that "yes" I knew He wanted. Something was keeping me from my total peace. I was like the person who gets out of jail and less than six months later is right back inside for the same offense.

While I had slowed down on the liquor and substances, I was still a slave to something far worse: people. That dependence opened the door to the chaos and confusion I was trying to detangle and be freed from in the first place. I let loyalty become slavery. I let my emotions and allegiance to people become an idol. I still felt this burning need to be a people pleaser. I had this need to feel important in order to feel complete. I still needed to feel needed and loved by everybody when I had already experienced a taste of where all the love I would ever need comes from. But it wasn't enough. I still wanted to be liked by everybody, forgetting that I was already liked by who mattered the most—God.

I chose people over God.

People pleasing and wanting validation through friends and strangers was at the core of why I didn't have peace. Making decisions based on what other people felt or said or might say was exactly what got me my problems. It would continue until I was delivered from it. This was a root that had to be dug up and dug out, otherwise, it would continue to grow back and grow back stronger each time.

This people pleasing and making choices based on other people was like growing bamboo. I had wild bamboo growing in my life, sprouting in every direction. Bamboo is an interesting plant. Well, it's not that interesting in its physical characteristics, just in the way that it grows… at least to me.

In the backyard at the house where I grew up, there was a whole field of bamboo. It had been growing long before we got there and the owner before us didn't keep up with it. No matter how many times my dad mowed that bamboo down, it always grew back. I remember watching my parents try every kind of weed killer and plant control product they could find. The bamboo just kept growing back more and more aggressively and it started to spread from the back to the sides of the house. It was unruly, unkempt and such an eyesore. It was also very costly to continue to try to suppress and get rid of. They spent thousands of dollars because our home served a dual purpose. It was our home, but it was also the church building.

After months and months, my dad came across some very pertinent and liberating information one day. He learned how bamboo grows and discovered how to get rid of it. We learned that simply cutting the bamboo at the surface would not get rid of it, but only allow it space to grow back. In order to get rid of that bamboo, it had to be killed at the root. It grew in a zigzag like pattern and had to be cut in the pattern in which it grew. The roots bended and twisted and took on various shapes underground. There wasn't one direction or angle that those roots grew. If we just touched the surface, we actually created better chances for it to spread more wildly. It had to be destroyed from the inside out, from underground to the surface. The entire backyard had to be dug up. It was a dramatic and tedious process, and it was expensive, but not as expensive, wasteful or pointless as other options had been. The entire plot of land where the bamboo grew had to be overturned, the roots dug up and destroyed.

This same process had to happen to me spiritually and mentally. I had to be overturned. I had things festering and growing on the inside in every direction. Feelings I couldn't explain. Everything and anything made me angry and depressed. God had to pull a whole lot of stuff out of me. Everything had to come up and be exposed. That night of revival was me finding out my life was full of chaotic bamboo. The days and nights to come would be me killing my "bamboo" at its core. It would cost me and it would require I made choices about what I was willing to lose in order to gain what I needed. I was about to find out how serious God is about being unable to serve two masters and the day coming wherein I had to choose.

My day came.

A hard choice had to be made. That choice was painful, but it brought me peace. In the process of pain and sacrifice, I found peace. I ended up having to let people go who I loved, people who I thought were down for me. In some cases, I had to let go people who actually were down for me, but I still had to let them go. I had to walk away from the very thing I wanted so badly. It was hard for me, but I finally found what I'd been really and truly missing: wholeness.

Chapter 9

And Then, When You're Still Finding...Yet Trying to Keep That Piece of Peace

When I got saved that night, I assumed everything would magically get better. I assumed that because I felt so relieved in that revival service. Surely, in the days to come, *poof*—all my problems would disappear and life would become this grand event.

That was the furthest thing from the truth then and it's still the furthest thing from the truth.

I had this feeling, sort of a spiritual high, from that night. I formulated this unrealistic expectation upon leaving that service because I felt so good at that moment. I was all set. This time would be different. I felt something shift on the inside of me and was sure all my problems would instantly cease to exist.

That is not how being a Believer works. It is a process. You'll never be a hundred percent complete until you reach the other side and get to Heaven. Coming to Christ is like a detoxification process, but it is a continuous detox. A full detox of the body takes time, and so does the process of purging the world from your life once you come to Christ. I expected everything wrong about me would start turning into right. That was a terrible assumption and the source of more vexation and frustration. I thought, *why didn't my salvation work?* I went to the altar and I prayed the prayer. I was serious about changing my ways and everything had felt so good that night. I was sincere and yet I still didn't have it together. I did what I felt I had to do, which was tell my parents everything, and I was starting to do better, but something was missing. Something was not right.

That was because I had only just begun to peel back the layers. I had said yes, and invited Jesus into my heart, but He got only a piece of my heart. There were some parts that I wanted to keep for me. Yes, I was reading my Bible and praying and working on my relationship with God, but I still was not in compliance with what I knew was His will for my life. Sin isn't defined only by the obvious sins, like murdering, stealing and lying; disobedience is a sin, too. That one, disobedience, was my sin.

I was saved, but I was still in disobedience. I knew exactly what God wanted from my life, but I still had little seeds of guilt, selfishness and people pleasing which were keeping me from going after it. I was in a relationship with the Lord on paper, but in practicality, I was between two loves. I loved the Lord. I was sincere about Him and about changing my life for Him—to an extent—but I had a love for some people and things still. I still was in love with some of the ways of the world. I wanted Him on my terms and conditions, and it doesn't work that way. That is why I had no peace. That is why that spiritual high quickly faded and I felt like I was back to square one.

There's no possible way you can be on two teams at the same time, be loyal to both teams or perform at your best on both teams. It doesn't work in sports and it definitely doesn't work when it comes to spiritual growth and relationship with God. The beginning of my coming home experience, being no longer lost, was very pleasant. I was on fire for the Lord. I went back to church, read my Bible and prayed. I shut down the things I knew I wasn't supposed to do: partying, drinking, smoking and having sex...for a while. Then, the feeling faded and before I knew it, I was back into the very things I said I was no longer going to do.

Why? Because I allowed myself to be lured back in through the spirit and trap of people pleasing. I let my understanding of what loyalty and friendship meant and even the mechanics of how I personally would approach loyalty and friendship become a struggle for me. I let treating people how I wanted to be treated become a form of enslavement as I put others before myself...and before God. This would serve as one reason I backslid and found myself between a rock and hard place time and time again.

I got saved, but I found myself back in my same ways because I didn't give my whole heart. I didn't give a complete yes to God. I knew certain people in my life could no longer be in such close proximity yet I refused to be real with myself about it. I lied to myself and convinced myself I could have my cake and eat it, too. I could serve God and still be close with those certain people, couldn't I?

No, sadly, I really couldn't. I tried and failed terribly.

In my heart, I knew I was going to go into ministry eventually. That was the calling on my life, but I didn't want to. I could already see where God was directing me and I fought against it. The path God had for me would mean cutting off friends I'd had for years. It would mean cutting off two particular friends who I loved very much and to whom I felt such strong allegiance. I just couldn't do that. Somehow I was going to find a way to serve God and to continue my life.

I convinced myself I could discipline myself so I didn't do the "bad" things anymore. I convinced myself, reasoning that I could be saved and just go with the flow. I wanted what I wanted and would do what was necessary to make it happen, if it was the last thing I did. I wanted to be just one of the church goers, a regular attendee. I wanted to do my good deeds, here and there, and lay low.

I fought with God and constantly asked, "Why do I have to be on the front lines?" I knew what being on the front lines would cost and what it would mean and the thought of that caused me to hesitate and run further from my call. My complete and total yes to God would cost me longtime friendships and associations, isolation and separation. It would require completely leaving everything familiar and trusting the process.

The biggest sacrifice was the severing of friendships. A definition of a friend to me is someone who has seen the worst possible things about you and who sticks around through them. By that definition, I had few friends, few people who had been down for me through my toughest of times.

There were two particular friends beside Imani who have been very significant in this process and my journey. In this process, I've become more and more thankful for these friends because of how I've grown. Had everything unfolded a different way, I wouldn't be the person I am today. For that, I cherish them no matter how ugly it once was between us. The good news is our friendships are not ugly anymore.

Tee was one of those friends. He had been down for me for several years. During the brief time I felt I had nobody else and nobody understood me, our friendship blossomed. He and I became friends at the end of tenth grade in 2007. In eleventh grade, when my world turned upside down, he was there. We were strictly friends. It was never anything sexual. We were best friends, brother and sister.

We used to cut up so bad on MySpace, Twitter and AIM (AOL Instant Messenger). That's how long and far back we go. We go back to Sidekicks and Blackberry BBM days. We were Bonnie and Clyde to each other and to everyone who knew us. Our friendship was one of codependency, although not in a negative sense. We had each other's back. We often put the battery in each other's back and tag-teamed things. At one point in our lives, when we both were making serious life decisions, we turned to each other for non-judgmental, sincere, pure-hearted help.

Like me, Tee grew up in church and around the same principles and standards for Godly living as me, and just like me, Tee came to a point in his life when he was trying to find himself and find his way. We ended up being the only people who understood the other person's situation when we both came to the threshold of a dramatic life turn.

My allegiance to Tee came from him being the sole person who 100% supported my choice not to keep my baby and understood why I made my choice. In that time, I needed someone to try to understand where I was coming from. I needed someone to see that although it was the wrong choice morally, I still needed a shoulder to lean on, a shoulder on someone who was going to be there to hold my hand because my parents weren't able to and didn't even know. I felt I was alone, but I had Tee.

It turned out, I was that for him, too. Our relationship was reciprocal. We hung out so frequently, Tee's family became my second family. I didn't know the time would come when I would need the same exact thing from him that I'd tried my best to give to him when he needed it most. Tee ended up giving back the loyalty I'd given to him and for that, to this day, I'm grateful. Even though a lot has changed for me and about me, I know I always have a place to go if I need one because when I needed one, I had a place to go.

Tee was not like the other boys I had known. He was heavily into fashion, more than the average man, and into entertainment. At times, he was my personal stylist. We couldn't leave the house or go out just any kind of way. My bestie was not having that. If you were with him, you were going to look like you were with him. And look the bomb. We always had to be extra fly. Sometimes we did corny stuff like match, but one thing was for sure: we always dressed when we stepped out. We called ourselves Beyoncé and Jay-Z—minus the relationship part. (We were so corny back then.) The way they stunt together was how we used to stunt together. Always. On. Point.

To me, our friendship was normal. We were two best friends who had similar interests, and I never thought anything of it until one day he confided in me just how different he was from the other guys. Tee was different because he liked guys. He came out to me; he was gay.

Deep down, I think I always knew it, but it was not something we'd ever discussed. It was something he had been struggling with for a while and finally had come to terms with. Oh, how familiar that feeling would be for me not long after this time. His pronouncement shocked me, but at the same time, it didn't. Immediately, I had mixed emotions. We both grew up in a faith which believes the Bible clearly says homosexuality is wrong, it is sin—it is missing God's best. Yet, in my heart, that belief never changed the way I felt about him. In fact, his coming out made us closer and drew me more to him.

I knew what it felt like to feel caged, a prisoner in your own body. I knew what it felt like to pretend to be one thing when on the inside you feel like another. I knew what it felt like to pretend just to save face, for the sake of others. I had been faking it for years, a good little church mouse, when havoc and chaos were slowly unraveling and about to explode in my own life very soon.

Naturally, although I knew Tee's lifestyle choice went against everything we grew up believing, that didn't change my love and care for him as a friend. I ended up helping him through the "coming out" process. Until he was ready to go public and tell his family and other friends, I was there for Tee. I never, ever threw the Bible at him—and still don't because it's not my place. We all have sins, and no sin is more excusable than another.

We all have an instinctual sense of right and wrong. While I'm very clear and concise on what I believe to be morally and ethically right, I try my best not to force that understanding upon other people because neither heaven nor hell belong to me and I can't put people in them. My true conviction is that while I can and will boldly speak truth and what God has outlined in His Word, I can never condemn those who aren't following that Word because there were many times I wasn't following it. That was my attitude back then, and it's still my attitude now.

Prom time came around. I agreed to be Tee's date without thinking twice because he wasn't able to take his significant other. People already speculated that we were a couple; some swore we were, but just very private about it. It was not even like that. This was about covering my best friend and being peace in a stormy situation. Pretending and covering for him was protecting my brother.

Watching my bestie be torn between the lifestyle he was living in secret and wanting to be free was like looking in the mirror. The circles my parents were known in looked at me like this Goody Two-shoes, expecting me to be perfect. I grew tired of pretending to be perfect. Just once, I wanted the chance to be accepted for me.

I understood Tee's dilemma. He got tired of pretending to be one way when he really was another. After he confided in me about his sexual orientation and after prom had come and gone, he told me he wanted to tell his family. I knew that was going to be major. I wanted him to be sure. I was ready to support whatever decisions he made.

When he actually let his sexual orientation be known, I was right there. His family still loved and embraced him, and even loved me for being a good friend. I unconditionally showed myself friendly because it was the right thing to do. Although I never enabled his lifestyle, I didn't preach fire and brimstone. That wasn't what he needed from me. He needed an ear, a confidant, so that's what I became.

That season came and went, and he was happier. That was all it was about for me back then—seeing the people I loved happy, even if their happiness affected what I personally believed. This became a pattern. Unfortunately, it often meant compromising myself and my standards, and although it wasn't right, I rationalized that if people I loved were happy, then my sacrifice wasn't in vain. As long as people liked me, I was okay. As long as people were happy with me, everything was okay.

See how the seeds of people pleasing can grow in our lives? That's how it grew like wild bamboo in me.

My turn came shortly after Tee's coming out. Even though I took tons of those Clearblue Easy Reader pregnancy tests—and they all said the same thing—some part of me still wished it was all a bad dream. Once reality set in and I realized the clock was ticking, I began to wrestle with the big choice. From beginning to end, Tee was there for me. I forever cherish him for that, and always will.

To explain just how close Tee and I were, let me tell you about one of the darkest days of my life: the day I terminated my pregnancy.

I can remember breaking the news to Tee. He was shocked and he asked me if I was sure. I took out the medium sized zip-lock bag that had several tests I took and nodded that I was sure. He asked me what I was going to do. He knew the dynamics of my relationship with my baby's father at the time and knew it was going to be bad for business if I followed through with this. But he also knew me and how I was raised. He knew like I knew that abortion shouldn't even have been an option for me and yet here I was considering it. When I finally decided which way I was going to approach it, he held my hand and let me know everything was going to work out in the end.

I had explored my options and carefully, without leaving a trail, I'd found two other clinics beside my local Planned

Parenthood. I knew off the top I didn't want to go there because it was too close to home and someone could have possibly seen me tip in or out. That was not a chance I was willing to take.

The first option didn't even end up being an alternative like it advertised. I asked Tee to drive me there just in case anything should happen, and he agreed. We went together. When we arrived at the destination, we were both surprised to find not a clinic or medical building, but a well-kept home with a green lawn and beautiful glass windows. I later learned it was the home of an older, Latino Christian woman. I assumed when I saw her advertisement as an "alternative women's option center" that meant clinic. Little did I know that I was walking into an emotional ambush.

Tee stayed in the car and waited for my call or my return to the car. I didn't make him come into the house with me, but I wish that I had. I rang the doorbell and waited anxiously. A short, stumpy Latino woman with glasses came to the door, opened it and let me in. She motioned for me to go up the stairs to the upper level of the house. My stomach sank deeper and deeper just thinking about how I had even gotten here. I was thankful I had Tee not too far away because my parents had no idea where I was. In their minds, Tee and I were at the mall just doing what we usually did on our spare time. They had no idea I was about to walk into an all-out showdown. I myself had no idea what I was walking into.

Not only was this place not what I expected on the outside in terms of the structure of the building, it was not what I expected on the inside either. I walked up the stairs and followed the woman to a room that was set up like an office. I saw nothing but anti-abortion paraphernalia, pamphlets, and all sorts of reading material. Everywhere. She had posters that said "Murderer," "Hell awaits you," "Repent" and all kinds of other material that terrified me and made me feel worse than I did.

I wondered if God even was present in that moment, but looking back I know He was because He is Omnipresent. He is everywhere, even in the most hellish of situations. A man said that one time in the Bible too. He said if he made his bed in hell, God would still be there. I had definitely made mine and I couldn't see it back then, but He was still with me and this was part of His plan. Though my situation clearly wasn't His perfect will for my life, it was His permissive will and He allowed it to happen for my good.

I can remember going into the room that was set up like an office. It was so cold and felt so dreary. I could feel the judgment in the woman's eyes as she stared at me. She opened a drawer and pulled out this sort of chart that you had to manually adjust and turn. She asked me when my last menstrual cycle was and I told her. She calculated and told me how far along I was and when my due date was going to be. She started talking to me as if I was preparing for the baby. She began telling me I had to physically and spiritually prepare and cleanse myself for me and my baby's sake. She had a tone about her that was so sneering and overpowering, like I had no choice but to have this baby. She was telling me all the things I would have to do, but I interrupted her.

I asked, "What if I'm not going to keep my baby?"

That set her off. She screamed, "Then you're going to be a murderer! Then you'll burn in hell. You already fornicated and wasted your treasure. Why don't you at least attempt to do right by your kid and make something of yourself for the kid? Although born through abomination, the child can still have a chance!" She tossed some pamphlets at me and screamed that abortion is murder and murder will send me to hell. "YOU'RE GOING TO HELL. STRAIGHT TO HELL!"

That's all I can remember her shouting over and over and over. It sounded like a death sentence had been spoken over me. A seed of trauma and ill words had been spoken.

I got so frightened I burst in tears. I cried hysterically. I got up from my side of the desk to leave and she tried to stand in my way. Angry, I violently mushed her out my way and offered her some colorful choice words which I will not repeat here before I ran down the stairs and out the door to Tee's car. He was parked and actually asleep in the car. I startled him with my banging on the window and hysterical tears. All I could do was weep in the passenger seat.

Tee begged me to explain what happened and even reached under the car seat for something like he was going to go back inside and haul off on whoever and whatever upset me. The way he did it was comical and helped me to laugh in the middle of my tears and pain.

I calmed down just enough to tell him what had happened, but recalling it caused the heavy tears to flow again. My heart was so heavy. How I wished I could go back to the night my child was conceived and change my mind. But I couldn't and this was my reality.

Tee hugged me so tight until I stopped crying. He told me over and over it would be okay. He told me that he loved me and no matter what, he would be there for me. All I could do was cry. I was terrified at the thought of hell being my eternal destination and now I was faced with making a choice that someone told me would send me there. I didn't understand at that time that it wouldn't be the abortion itself that would send me to hell. It would be closing my eyes without having truly repented to God for it that would send me there. Herein is where I came to the most irrational, Level 5000 dumb conclusion. I concluded that if this was already hell on earth for me, then I didn't have to make it hell on earth for anyone else. And I wasn't going to. I would suffer now and just suffer whatever else would come later. There was no easy way out and I thought I was taking the lesser of two evils.

Chapter 10

Having to Say "Peace Out"

to Let Peace In

I clearly thought wrong at that point because from there on out, things got progressively worse. Had I not had my best friend there by my side to support me, suicide could very well have been another option I chose. Only once did I consider it and that was the day of the actual procedure. After it was done, I immediately regretted what I had done.

Tee's words that day were so comforting. He kept reassuring me I was going to be okay. His words helped but I was still pregnant and still had to follow through with what I planned to do because time was running out. It was getting harder to hide and to lie about. Not only were morning sickness, cravings and mood swings becoming harder to hide, my belly was getting harder to hide and by law, pregnancies are allowed to be medically terminated only up to 24 weeks.

When the day came for me to have the abortion, I was a little bit past that point. I ended up going into New York City to a low-end, back alley place to have the procedure. I had heard about it through a girl in my gym class who noticed my bump one day while we were changing. I did my research on how to get there, the cost, etc. and it panned out that she was right about it. It seemed reputable. It seemed clean and safe. She was an expert at this sort of thing and from what I knew of her, a frequent and a satisfied customer. I don't know where she is today, but often I think of her and hope she's okay. I went through that one time and know what a toll it took on me physically, emotionally and spiritually. I can't imagine what it has done to her having gone though it several times. The only person I can speak for and give an account for is myself, though, and thus, I can truly say grace hovered over me through that process because I could have died on that operating table. I could have died and wouldn't have had anyone to be accountable for me—not even Tee. Even his sticking by me had a limit.

Through that whole period and process, the one Person who never left me was the same Person I ran from and lashed out against for so long. Where family and friends who didn't intentionally fail me, but who did couldn't reach, God has been able to reach and He snatched me out. If you are reading this and can relate, then please understand when I tell you that He for sure can snatch you out of whatever you are going through, too. He heals the brokenhearted, the wounded, the devastated and the grief-stricken. I was all of those things, and God has healed me.

Tee came with me to this facility. He again drove me because I had to have someone with me and well, who else was going to go? I skipped out on school that day to have it done and had my alibi in place. Of course, my parents never found out that day, but they had their suspicions when I came home that I had been involved in something not quite right.

The place was a rundown building and it did not look as grand as that girl from gym class hyped it up to be. But I went in anyway. I was too far along (no pun intended) to turn back. This time, Tee went in with me. I was ready to get it over with and just go home. I filled out some papers of some sort that asked me questions and I remember signing some type of disclosure. I don't remember everything it said except I was giving consent to anesthesia and drugs. I zoomed through those papers because I wanted it over with. That was the last place I wanted to be. I had not eaten because I had been instructed not to or else I couldn't get the anesthesia, so I was very hungry.

There were so many other girls there—Black, white, Latino. We all looked lost and confused. I could tell some had been there before, but some were just like me...regretful. The sickening scary thing was seeing a girl I knew from the church where my father was employed as Minister of Music. She wasn't just a random girl from the choir, though. She was like a foster daughter to the choir director who was very close with my dad. We were very familiar with each other. Although she didn't recognize me in my incognito shades and hoodie, I recognized her. I was disappointed in her because she already had a daughter and she wasn't taking care of that one. I self-righteously felt she hadn't learned her lesson. She should not have been there.

How crazy is that? I was mad at someone for doing the very same thing I about to do. I really should have been mad at myself instead of looking to point out the faults of others. I was silently pointing my finger with three others pointing straight back at me. I looked around at the other people there. Each and every woman was young, mostly minority, and unwed, judging by our empty ring fingers. Some were there with other girls and others, if not most, had a male with them. I imagined and assumed those girls were with their significant others, judging by body language, heads leaning on shoulders and intertwined hands. I, however, was not. I was with my gay best friend.

When that reality hit me, I shed a few tears, but quickly wiped them away so as to not make a big scene. I was there for one thing and one thing only, and it wasn't to feel sorry for myself. It was to be a big girl and handle the issue at hand. I was sad because I felt like my boyfriend/baby's father –whatever he was at the time since we were on and off—should have been there with me. It hurt and angered me that he wasn't, and that I was alone. Of course, I wasn't alone literally because Tee was there and I am grateful that he was, but I was still alone in the sense that the person I had gotten into all this trouble with wasn't there. Sure, he had chipped in to help me come up with part of the $900 expense, but the brunt of all this was falling on me. I was the one there handling it. I was the one who had been lying and sneaking. I was the one who was sick in the mornings. It was all me and that hurt because I didn't get myself pregnant.

I vowed that day not to ever have sex again which would be a complete lie, but I remember how horrible I felt in that moment and I told myself if this was what sex got me, they could keep it. It wasn't worth all the emotions I was feeling and how uncomfortable and hard it was for me. It wasn't worth it then, and it's still not worth it now. Although God heals and restores you from traumatic experiences, you never ever forget them. You learn and get the grace to move past them, which I have. But having an abortion is a choice I will never forget for the rest of my life. Thankfully, I'm whole enough now to be able recall it and share it in a way that hopefully someone else becomes whole, too.

Although I felt alone compared to those other girls who had their dudes with them, I had my A-1, Day 1 with me, and he had brought along his friend. They were so supportive of me. They constantly asked if I was okay and reassured me that all would be alright. Tee especially made sure he did everything he could to make sure I was comfortable or as best as I could be. He stayed with me.

I went in and did it. In that low-down, rinky dink clinic. What I did was irreversible. What was done was done. The anesthesia put me out so I don't remember everything, but I remember becoming conscious, getting dressed to leave and immediately feeling the repercussions of what I had done. Not only did I start to feel physically sick, a little part of me died there right along with my child. My spirit was crushed, but hey, it was over, right? Problem was solved.

Wrong.

My problems were only beginning. I was about to be in for the ride of my life. But that's life, isn't it? You just deal with it. That's what society teaches us, to simply get over it. That's what I told myself I had to do. I had to get over it and be a big girl now. I did what I did and there was nothing else to say. I did it with the mentality that nobody else would be hurt from this but me and I could hide it and nobody would ever know.

The surgeon told me, give or take a week, in about a month, I would be healed. I could go back to my normal activities. He gave me some prescriptions and sent me on my way so he could prepare to handle the next patient. Just like that I was wheeled out to the waiting room and sent home.

I felt so broken. Tee was there to pick up the pieces. He was the first person I saw. Emotionally, I latched on to him, and I started to feel like I owed him. I owed him from here on out and I promised him I would be there for him if he ever needed me. I didn't realize there would come a time, years down the line, when I would have to choose between my promise to him and God. I would come to a place where I had to cut someone so close to me while in search of truly finding God. What a rollercoaster ride that would be.

The days that followed took a toll on me physically, mentally, emotionally and spiritually. Physically, I got a bacterial infection from not having the proper medications. Emotionally, I was a wreck. Spiritually, I was lifeless. I started avoiding church and God all together. I felt so dirty and I was sure God was done with me. My years of partying, drinking, lashing out and seeking attention all stemmed from this one incident: a one-time event that had recurring repercussions. I had no peace and looked for any and every escape from the trauma of what happened.

I faked the funk to all my friends, even Tee. Tee and I partied together in straight and gay clubs more times than I can count.

At one point, it was a weekly thing for us. For him, it was just going out for fun, but for me, it was a coping mechanism. At the end of the liquor bottles and rolled blunts, I was still faced with my hard reality. I needed help and I needed help badly.

Well, from the flow of this book, you know I actually went to the threshold of getting that help when I gave my heart to Christ, but it meant I had to make some choices. Really and truly, a person cannot be hot and cold at the same time. I really wanted my identity, my sense of belonging and my peace, and I had to be in Christ to get them. Letting go of friendships that didn't reflect Godly living was inevitable and urgent. Tee and I would have to separate.

I fought that decision for so long. I thought just because I had chosen this path toward God didn't mean he had to or that we couldn't be friends. Looking back, I can say had I just listened when God said to separate myself the first time, our later problems and falling out could have been avoided.

I let my loyalty to Tee as a result of him being there through my hardest place become an emotional burden and prison for me. I wanted him to continue to be my best friend no matter what. If that meant trying to juggle him and God, I would. For quite some time, I sat on the fence, still doing the things we did before I got saved, only to turn around and repent. It was premeditated sin, all because I didn't want to lose my best friend.

Had I listened when I got saved in 2013 and immediately began to weed out people and things not aligned with His plan for me, I could have saved myself countless tears and arguments. I wanted Tee and me to be just the way we used to be, but *I* was no longer the way I used to be.

A change was happening. He felt it as much as me. It caused us to beef with each other. I no longer wanted to drink, but I still came around. To me, I was just eager to be in his company and hang out. To him, I was being a killjoy, and worse, boring and uninteresting, not to mention my worst fear, judging. He felt I was judging him because he still liked to do the things I no longer wanted to do. We had spats which often left us not speaking for periods of time. That hurt me and made me question God. It angered me and made me talk to Him as if it were His fault when I was the one who had not listened when told to stay free now that I was free. I was the one who let the pleasing of friends become entrapment.

Even in that time, God was gracious to me and gave me a way out. It wasn't easy, but it was a way out. That's what "sufficient grace" is all about. It is not about being the easy way; it's about meeting the need all the way.

Tee wasn't the only friend in my party turn up circle who didn't like the change in me, but he had the hardest time accepting or embracing it, and that took a toll on our friendship. We became awkward around each other. Once best friends, we became like strangers. I cried so many tears, not understanding why my best friend couldn't support or understand I had finally found something worth holding on to, something that made sense of all the chaos in my life, my head and my heart.

What I failed to realize was God was taking me through the severing of emotional ties and teaching me how to lean on Him and Him alone. God was guiding me through the severing process to fully restore my joy and my peace. My friendship with Tee was a significant portion of this process, but it was only one portion. I learned to walk alone and soul search for who I am because I am independent of any other person. My identity and sense of belonging or peace can never come from another person. I had to get comfortable being alone. It was awkward. I no longer had loads of people I could call up to hang out with. Imani was preparing to get married and live her life. Tee and I couldn't hang out.

I felt very much alone.

This loneliness forced me to my knees to cry out and pray and pick up my Bible and read. There were nights I was tempted to get up and get dressed to go out to the club because I felt so alone, but I forced myself to stay in the house and read my Bible and pray, to sit still in silence and meditate on God's word. I had to give myself room to cry. It was during this period when I moved out of my parent's home, also to help me find myself. I deleted my Instagram account and went into full isolation. I disappeared because I needed God to really work on my emotions and kill that bamboo root of people-pleasing that had grown uncontrollably in my life. It's at the point when we willingly die to self that Christ can truly take over.

Dying to self meant letting go of friendships I had had for years and accepting the fact that people change and grow apart. I had to accept I was on a different path and that was okay. I had to accept this was and forever would be the road less traveled. To this day, I still walk alone in some areas although I have awesome friends in the kingdom of God. Finding and keeping peace started to come—and eventually stayed—when I stopped trying to force things and let God work. Peace started to come when I gave myself room to grieve as God severed emotional and soul ties of that friendship. Just because people have been in your life for a certain number of years doesn't mean they will be around for all of your years. Peace of heart, mind and spirit came when I decided to trust God with the process.

I walked away from the fast life and my friends and stopped looking back. I promised God I would do it His way after it became obvious doing it my way kept failing. I promised I would stop being on the fence and running from my call, but I had a request. It was my heart's desire. I prayed constantly that God would touch Tee's heart and those of all my other friends to understand it really wasn't them; it was me. I wanted Him to show them I needed to find me and find Him. I prayed and activated my faith that in time we would reconcile and become cordial again. I prayed and trusted that if I let go, God would do the rest and make it all worth it.

There's a reason why Jesus only requires us to have a mustard seed-sized faith. He only needs a little bit to work with to make the biggest change and impact in our lives. At no doing of my own, my old friends and I reconciled some time later. Shockingly, they came to me. My consistency, when I finally started to walk in obedience and answer my call, got their attention. God granted my small request.

Tee and I reconciled, and although he and I still live two different lives and are on two different paths, we have gotten to a place where we are able to talk to each other without tension. Things aren't the way they used to be between us, but we are starting to be back in each other's lives. I know my prayers about it and for him paid off. I know my consistency upon choosing this path, yet still extending love from afar, paid off. There were times I sent him encouraging words and Scriptures to tell him I loved him. It all worked. Loving him still as a friend from that isolated, insulated place let him see I was the same Adara; I just did things differently now. I was and still am the same crazy nut who loved to dance, but my reason for dancing has changed. I'm still the life of the party, getting everybody hyped, but now I'm hyped too and I'm not faking it. I'm still partying; it's just these days, it's a Holy Ghost party.

Perhaps this part of my journey is your current situation or reality. You're at a place where you have to choose. I want to encourage you to choose wisely and choose boldly. Don't be afraid of letting go of friendships or any kind of relationships to be close to God. Even Jesus had to do so. There came a point when He needed God the most, in that isolated place in the garden of Gethsemane. His twelve friends, twelve brothers, couldn't go with him. There comes a time—actually more than one time—when it has to be just you and the Lord. Embrace it. I know it's hard and it might not seem fair. Trust me, I get it, and Jesus gets it too. Those were His sentiments exactly when He prayed to God and asked that if there were any way He could skip the suffering, but He also prayed no matter what, that God's will be done. That's the kind of prayer we ought to pray. Yes, we can pray and go to God with our desires, but ultimately, we should want what He wants for us.

Here's a prayer you can pray regarding finding and keeping the peace in your life:

Lord, I ask that You give me the strength and courage to choose you. I know I can't cheer on two teams. Give me the courage to make up my mind to serve You wholeheartedly. It is my desire to honor You and make You smile with my whole life, including my thoughts, actions, speech and relationships or friendships. I pray You show me those things and/or people I may have to withdraw from or discontinue associating with in order to choose you. I thank You for choosing me and not thinking twice about it.

Lord, help me to maintain my peace in You. No matter what people think or say or feel, help me to remember what You say, think and feel as it is written in Your Word. Help me to trust this process of cleansing and purging that You have me under. In your Word, it says You know the plans you have for me, to give me hope and a future, according to Jeremiah 29:11. I trust Your plans. I know You have my best interest at heart and so, I pray now and surrender my heart and every area of my life to receive and remain in Your peace.

In Jesus' name, I pray,

Amen.

Well, that is a start to finding and keeping your peace. While it won't be easy and it will cost you a sacrifice, it is worth it. Sacrifice is the nature of love. It is the nature of the love of Jesus, and Jesus is worth it. Jesus thought and still thinks *you* are worth it. If I could encourage you and convince you to believe the same, then I've done my job. I would never tell you this is a cakewalk because it's not. It's a faith walk. Faith is a confidence and gentle reassurance in what you cannot see. It's going to take faith to go through this process. Trust it is worth it and ultimately, it ends up being for your good.

I found peace when I surrendered what I wanted and traded it in for what God wanted. My story doesn't stop here with the severing of friendship ties and choosing Him. In other ways, I was still a prodigal, but I was on the journey to finding my way and that peace grew more meaningful.

That is ultimately what you want. A meaningful walk and relationship with Jesus. It can be yours if you want it...but only if you want.

Love, *Adara*

Chapter 11

Then There's This Thing Called Finding, Getting and Giving Forgiveness

What is forgiveness?

If you had to define it, how would you define forgiveness? Why do we need it, if we do? Who does it benefit? These are all questions I can remember my father asking us one time when we were having a family meeting in our home. (Yes, we had "town hall" or family meetings to update each other, address major life changes and events, spend time together and hold family court on whatever issues were thwarting the sacred peace of our home.) Although I can't remember the reason for this particular town hall, I vividly remember going around the living room and us each having to speak about forgiveness. I'm sure there had been some sort of fight among the siblings. If it reached town hall status, it was important.

We all went around, then it came time for my answer. My reply was forgiving someone is to pardon the wrong they've done without excusing it, but at the same time, not holding on to it. I didn't even understand the true nature of forgiveness back then. Over the course of my twenty-five years on this planet so far, I've since learned what it means to get as well as to give forgiveness and just how important it is to our lives.

One of the things I love most about the prodigal son story is the way forgiveness is such an intricate part of the story. Forgiveness was waiting on the son at the door— literally. The forgiving love of the father was for him, yes, but everyone in that story was touched or changed by forgiveness. Doesn't that sound familiar? All of us have the opportunity to be touched and changed by God's embrace and His love, if we just turn and come back to Him. Everyone was affected by the extension of grace and forgiveness by the father. Everyone reacted and experienced it in a different way. From the son to his older brother to even the father—everybody had a difference experience. That's how life is.

That's how we are all connected, and that's how and why our decisions never really belong solely to us. The cause and effect of our decisions are not limited to us. This is why people end up getting hurt in situations: cause and effect. There is a cause and effect to everything. Since decisions are never for one person, then forgiveness is really never for just one person.

In this particular story, forgiveness taught the prodigal son about himself and something about his father. Let's look at what the prodigal son learned about forgiveness. He learned that true forgiveness, just like true love, is unconditional. That's what I too learned in this process. I too learned my forgiveness from God as well as love from God and from my parents weren't predicated or built on anything I had done. They weren't predicated or built on anything I could do. Their unconditional love for me was built on the fact it was what was right and it was what I need. Grace and love will cover your needs. Sufficient, as in grace sufficient, is able to meet and to surpass your need.

I was forgiven.

The forgiveness I received definitely met my needs and was sufficient. Because I was forgiven, I am able to write this book. I got a do over and a fresh start. A "take two" even as the cameras of my life were rolling. It really was like "take 5000," but you get my point. I got another chance.

This prodigal princess got what she needed and you can too. Whatever you need can actually be yours. Forgiveness was what I needed most and quiet as kept, I still need it more than anything. I still mess up and fall short; I'm just not falling over the same things or tripping over my own feet, and that's the important thing to remember. You're never going to be perfect, so stop expecting to be. Perfection's too much of a burden to place on yourself when you'll never be able to reach it. You'll always be a work in progress, so allow yourself to be. Allow yourself the healing growth process that comes when you mess up—because you will—then allow yourself to be forgiven.

If necessary, do the forgiving. I had to and I'll get to that in just a few. Forgiving doesn't mean condoning someone's actions or making excuses for them, but it means allowing grace and love to cover whatever their fault or mistake. That's what the prodigal son's father did for him. He never excused what his son did nor pretended it didn't happen. He simply forgave him once the young man saw the error of his ways. Life humbled that prodigal son until he had nothing. He had to go back to the person he humiliated. He had to return home after striking out on his own as if he were big and bad. Again, that was me. I had to humble myself and ask for forgiveness from my parents and from God because, just like that prodigal son, I learned I truly wasn't all that poppin'.

Without God, we are not even close to poppin'. We can have status and money and a little shine, but those only last for so long, just as we see in that story. The prodigal's status—his clout, his money and the 'likes' of people—all ran out. All of mine ran out too. That humbled me. I tried so super hard to be "lit" and I failed horribly. I thought I needed the endorsement of people I knew and didn't know to make me something. I turned my back and traded in the love of the real people I knew for people I didn't know. I needed to be forgiven for that. I needed to acknowledge what was foully done.

The prodigal's older brother learned an interesting thing about extending forgiveness from this ordeal, too. We can never choose our family like we choose our friends, but I believe God chooses our families for us and places us where we need to be for our own good. God placed me in a family where I ended up with everything I needed, and this has worked out for my good. That prodigal son in the Bible too was in a family divinely orchestrated by God to be what he needed. Wherever God has placed you, it is for your good, no matter the current dynamics. Ultimately, it is part of a bigger picture and His plan.

My lessons about forgiveness didn't stop with me accepting Christ and starting to make amends with my family. I had to learn how to forgive the people who hurt me, and boy, that was hard for me. Chile... God was at work in my heart because I had deep-seated anger, bitterness and rejection that manifested in so many ways. Rejection, bitterness and unforgiveness were seeds I watered with my tears and tried to drown in my drinks. It never worked. Those seeds had to be cut out at the root so they could never again grow. I was bitter, hurt and angry, and I needed to let forgiveness work in my life—giving as much as getting. I needed to be free from emotional bondage.

I am now.

I had to learn to ask for forgiveness from people I didn't mean to hurt. Even though I didn't mean it, I was still responsible for making things right. Forgiveness plays a major part in my testimony because although I got saved and forgiven by God, true freedom came from letting go of what hurt me and making things right with all of the people I had hurt. Because that's the thing... It's human nature to not want to be accountable. We love to be the victim. We love to shy away from when we've been the violator. I loved to point fingers when it came to what was done to me and what I had to endure, but there came a point when I had to step back and reevaluate what I had done to others and how my actions affected them. Although everything was paid for on the cross, we still have a responsibility to make things right with the people in our lives.

Beside my friend Tee and my parents, another person who taught me important lessons about forgiveness is another friend of mine, Amar. Amar has seen every side of me: up and down, good and bad, even crazy. He watched me go through this process to find myself and God. He was there from the beginning of the changeover and is here still. We met when I was nineteen and we were both in college. To this day, neither of us is sure how we linked up with each other, but we are mutually glad we did.

Amar and I were close like best friends, but in this case, there also was a romantic interest there. On and off, from ages nineteen to twenty-three, we dated while having this bestie/boyfriend/girlfriend thing going on. We were alike in so many ways yet so different.

Amar grew up in a Christian family too, but he wasn't a pastor's kid like me. He was good people. He looked out for me not just because I was his shorty, but because he had a good heart. He was funny, intelligent and very handsome. Of course back then, I was into the physical attributes of a guy, and he was super cute. He was older than me and he was a ball player, so I was drawn to that, too. Amar was not like the boys I was used to, though. He was not the one to stroke my ego or be thirsty. He was very straightforward and blunt, and naturally, being a little bit older, he expected certain things of his woman.

He was not a fan of the excessive partying, drinking or stunting for The Gram and he let it be known. His thing was balance and moderation, and that I represented him. We began to fall into an on and off situation, and when we were off, I looked for the missing piece elsewhere. Amar checked me on it a few times, but back then, I was a know-it-all. This was my life. He would tell me when something was too much or went too far, but I did not care. I was not trying to hear that.

I liked the fact that I was getting attention and that I was lit. It gave me the validation I thought I needed. I took his feelings and attitude about my lifestyle to mean he didn't want me to have fun and that he was boring when the opposite was true. I see just how much he cared for me—by not arguing with me and letting me find my own way.

I had taken things too far. He was patient and laid back and let me do my thing. I know now that he realized I was trying to find myself, so he let me. He tried to steer me in the right direction, but I was not mature enough to see it. After being off and on for some time, we eventually stopped talking altogether. I ended up immediately getting into a relationship with someone else who attended my college. It was blatant and in Amar's face, and although I felt bad, slightly, in that time of my life, I was very selfish. I rationalized that what I did was honorable because I didn't cheat on him. I've never been a cheater. It was my philosophy then that it is more honorable to leave than to cheat. In reality, either way people are hurt and that's exactly what happened.

Everybody in that situation got hurt. Everybody. Especially Amar. He watched me flaunt the next guy in his face while I pretended to be happy. He watched me continue to dress less than ladylike and overindulge the "turn up queen" lifestyle. He watched, but never dissed me nor attempted to play me in return. He let me do me and still supported me from afar. I know

I hurt him because he later told me. What we had was more than a romantic interest. Feelings were invested. I met his family. He saw himself later down the line with me for the long run, but I hurt him by my actions.

Anything built on a shaky foundation will crumble and that's what happened with the guy for whom I curved Amar. To everyone on campus, from the outside looking in, we had the cutest little relationship. Behind closed doors, though, it was chaos and hell. We were the type of couple to post pictures like we were happy, but be arguing and cursing each other out like sailors when no one could see or hear us. The only time we were ever on good terms was when we were sexually intimate or drunk. Both of us were lost and using each other to fill the voids and try to mend our broken pieces. He was just as broken as me and we tried to soothe each other's wounds. It never worked. He and I ended up breaking up, getting back together, then breaking up again.

We were not meant for a relationship. We were so toxic for each other, but we stayed together trying to force it. No matter how broken the relationship was. No matter how much we were starting to dislike each other and argue. No matter how much skimpier and provocative I got. No matter how verbally abusive he got. He stayed. I stayed.

Two broken people will never be able to function well together. I learned that from this relationship. Sex caused more confusion in the relationship and led to more trust issues on top of the already huge trust issues we both had. He didn't trust me because I was so provocative and flirtatious and because I partied so much. I didn't trust him because I was insecure, needy and didn't know who I was. I swore up and down he was cheating without any real proof because I was insecure about myself.

Our relationship ended for good in 2013. The breakup was like hitting a pressure point and pushed me to the place where I started to find God. A few months after our very bad breakup, I gave my heart to God in that revival with Imani because I was tired and broken and had finally realized that jumping from this guy to that guy wasn't going to make me happy. Jumping from guy to guy was so damaging to me. I'm grateful today this particular ex and I have become cordial and he is in the process of finding the Lord for himself. I know now I had to be out of the picture for that to happen just as he had to be out of the picture for my change to happen.

When a relationship is not God-ordained, it will only last for so long. A relationship with someone else won't last when your relationship with God isn't where it needs to be. My relationship with God was *not* where it needed to be, so the cookie crumbled. We got fed up with each other, yes, but the fact is it was not God's will for us to be together and time was up. Sin complicates everything, so the severing process was brutal on both of us.

A soul tie is a physical, emotional and spiritual connection created when two people are intimate sexually with each other. The two individuals become one in spirit and in body and often take on each other's characteristics. They become joined together. The Bible is so clear on why intimacy and sex are designed for one man and one woman in marriage, because you become a part of each other. That's exactly what happened here. A soul tie was formed.

The soul tie that was created had to be broken and I had to be delivered. It didn't get broken right away. I didn't even know I had a soul tie to him until I realized I was competing for his attention and affection long after we had decided it was over. At the same time, I was seeking the affection of people I didn't even know to try to fill the hole in my heart. I was not acting like myself and reverted back to things that had happened in that relationship. I jumped from party to party, from this thing to that thing, all trying to fill the hole that kept getting bigger. The more I tried to fill it, the bigger it got. It became bigger than the baby I didn't keep. I was incomplete. I was empty and broken. I got so tired of faking it and so weary that I gave up. I needed God's help and decided to embrace it.

When I did sever that relationship, got saved and started my new journey, I knew immediately I had to make things right with Amar. I expected him to hate me and curve me, but he never did. He forgave me like nothing ever happened, probably in part because I had already experienced my payback for what I did to him. I know, however, it was really because he loved and cared for me and still does. Amar let me back in and didn't hold what happened over my head. Although we semi-tried to rekindle the old flame, and it worked for a little while, eventually our relationship crashed again. We were so good, almost too good, and it all came to an immediate halt for a second time when an even bigger problem arose.

I was no longer wilding out and hurtful in the way I had treated him before. This time, I hurt him by first trying to force him into marriage, then disappearing from his life for a second time shortly after that with no explanation. Although when I disappeared for the second time around, it was with valid reason, the way I went about it was wrong and I hurt him— again. Again, I needed to be forgiven and again he extended forgiveness to me when I asked for it. Later, we both would see how he needed things to happen this way. The events surrounding my life and my feelings forced him to take a look at some things where he was concerned, too.

Amar and I were not done. We started to be good again and we tried the couple thing once more. Eventually marriage came up in my head, but that was the issue. I was trying to marry a man who wasn't trying to marry me. Amar didn't want to marry me at the time that I wanted to be married. It wasn't because of the lifestyle I'd previously lived or because I was a bad person.

Never once did he look at me dirtily or like I was less of a woman. To him, I was still his dream girl and best friend, no matter had happened. It was because he wasn't ready and truthfully, I was not ready either. Both of our lives would have been destroyed had we married each other.

Although I loved Amar and he will make someone an awesome husband someday, I selfishly wanted him to be mine for all the wrong reasons. I wanted to be married so I could have all the sex I wanted guilt-free and without worrying about slipping up and falling. I wanted to be married for the wedding day itself and the diamond ring. I wanted to be married because people around me were getting married. And I wanted him to be my husband to fill a space he could never fill.

My best friend married young. I watched as family members got married young. I wanted that, too. I thought if we waited to be intimate and have sex, it would be okay since we hadn't been intimate for some time. It was my desire to be celibate. We weren't going to be intimate unless I changed my mind. He respected me and never tried to get me to break my celibacy.

I was so sure. We should have, could have and were going to get married. I was so sure of this. We'd already known each other for so long and we had a relationship. We could get married and stay married, right? Wrong.

First off, I had to learn that as a Christian, your spouse has to be God- ordained. Marriage is an institution created by God. He joined Adam and Eve together. He joins people together. That's why in the wedding vows the minister says words along the lines of "what God joins together, let no man—and that implies woman, FYI—tear apart or put asunder." God has to be at the center of your relationship and definitely of your marriage as a Believer, otherwise, it WILL NOT WORK. You can pick your mate yourself, but your marriage will not be blessed that way. If you wait on God and let Him choose for you and then send His confirmation to you, your marriage will be blessed.

The second thing I had to learn was that marriage is not like how it is presented by Disney. Marriage is work! It's hard work. You can't marry someone based on how they make your feel or how well you "click." There will come a time when you can't stand each other, when you're getting on each other's nerves to where you no longer want to be around each other. If you've married for any reason other than love and sacrifice, when that time comes, your marriage will fall apart because its foundation is shaky. I say this all the time, but it's my truth that I want a marriage where I continuously say "I do" even when I don't. Even when I don't want to because I know myself and there will be times I want to be alone.

I had no clue about marriage back then, yet I was hinting around it to Amar. I wasn't content with being a single, unmarried woman, and thus, other issues started to uproot within me. I thought a husband would make me happy. I thought a husband was essential to me being a woman. Both are the farthest thing from the truth. Not every woman will be married. Not being married or not ever marrying doesn't make you less of a woman. I had to learn this. I learned it in my isolation period, the period of time where I cut off friends to learn how to get content and stay content with just the Lord and His Word. It was hard for me and there were growing pains, but they made me into who I am now: a woman complete in Christ and satisfied with Him because Heaven, not a husband nor a boatload of friends, is my life goal. I've been set free and I plan to stay free from some serious bondage.

In my isolation period, I severed my relationship/friendship with Amar. I blocked his number so I wasn't tempted to call him or answer his calls. I knew he would try to figure something out for us to find common ground. I blocked him because I couldn't tell him that we couldn't be together. I would sound quite crazy trying to explain that I needed to be alone to heal from him not wanting to marry me and me not being wife material. He would have called the psychiatric hotline to have them come get me if I had continued on and told him then I soon would be going into ministry to preach because God had told me to. There was no way to explain it logically because any explanation would only make things worse.

How can you forewarn someone about torrential, life-altering, Jumanji-like rain coming into your life? How do you tell then to prepare for it without worrying or scaring them off? I didn't want to do that to him because he wouldn't have understood. Beyond that, I didn't know how to express correctly everything that was happening with me...because I didn't know everything that was happening. He was going to be hurt and confused again. Again I left his life abruptly.

Cutting off Amar was so hard for me, but I had to do it. I had already seen what happened with Tee when I tried to juggle conflicting emotions and straddle the fence to do things my way. I remembered how I backslid trying to do that. I saw the tension it caused with my friends. I had learned that lesson and I wasn't about to repeat it, so I cut him off. I needed him to be out of sight, mind and heart so I could purge and learn how to lean on only God, to hunger for just God and not any man. Amar needed me to be out of the picture so when we returned to each other's lives, he would understand how God works in people and be able to begin that journey to God for himself. Again, I faced a time of humbling myself and I had to apologize to one of the hearts I broke while I healed and fixed mine. Although I regret not letting him know he wasn't the problem, that it was me, I don't regret the process or the actual isolation because we both grew from and healed from it.

We went well over a year, close to two, without speaking to each other. In early 2015, I reached out to Amar via Instagram DM. I wasn't sure if he had blocked my number like I had blocked his. I was the last person he wanted to talk to. Twice I had walked out of his life like it was nothing, like he was of no importance or value to me. I prayed he would read the DM and listen to my heart speak. In that message, I told him everything, from Tee and I to accepting the call to ministry. I opened up about the nights in my apartment when it was just me, my Bible and the tears on my pillow. I shared how him not wanting to marry me forced me to evaluate myself and face the fact that I was never really about him. I had needed to go underground and away from him because I had some serious issues. I apologized and hoped he would answer. I would have understood and not been mad if he hadn't. Without being extra preachy, I gave a quick encouraging word and gave him my information in case he chose to speak to me and I left it there. He didn't reply right away, but when he did, it again was with love and understanding. He accepted my apology for waltzing away without explanation, then shared what my abrupt leaving did to and for him.

Although I had no idea how I would have gone about it then, he would have appreciated if I had given him something, some sort of explanation. My disappearing act left him hurt a second time. He assumed I had run off with someone else again which left him feeling a way that was less than pleasant. He explained how confused and troubled my actions left him, wondering what was it about us that really wasn't. It made him question marriage and whether it was for him because of the way it was presented and how I had approached him about it. My disappearing forced him to look at himself to figure out the man in the mirror and reevaluate some things in his own life. Amar had no idea of the change that had happened within me, but looking at my IG and my pictures, he could tell I was a totally different girl, that I had found myself. He liked this new me; he was feeling her. He said he literally could see and feel the difference. He forgave me for keeping him out the loop and not being open with him. He forgave me for hurting him and we became cool once again.

His response was yet again an answer to prayer. I prayed, "If this is You, God, and I let go, please let them see You and see the change in me as a result of this process." Not only did Amar start to experience God on another level for himself, he also took to the Bible and prayer much more in that period when we were not in communication with each other.

I'll never forget this one day he texted me. We were chatting and talking, and he said, "Like I told you before, you have this new energy about you that is crazy. You are meant to change someone's life on some serious stuff. Like watching your transition is crazy for me because I feel like I've known you forever." It did my heart good to read that text and see that everything had not been in vain.

Today, we are just as cool as we once were minus the romance part. That part of the relationship has since changed, but we are very good friends and any woman he dates has to go through the examination process and be deemed worthy before they can get together because he is a rare breed of man. (I'm kidding, sort of.) Amar helped me grow. He helped me by not wanting to marry me. I was forced to confront the marriage idol and unnecessary comparison of my life to other people's lives. He helped me gain the confidence I needed to make choices and decisions for me, yet be sure they don't hurt anyone rooting for me in the process. The lesson learned here was solidified for me because it came from a friend, not from my parents. Above all, he forgave me and has not mentioned even once the way I was selfish and haphazard with his feelings—twice. He proved to me forgiveness is never really just for you. It heals you, and when your heart is set on pleasing God, even if you don't get everything correct, love and grace still cover.

I asked for forgiveness and I was forgiven, but there was more.

Although I got my forgiveness, another key part of my journey from the prodigal back to the princess, another critical lesson I had to learn, was that I had some major forgiving to do of people who I felt really, truly did not deserve my forgiveness and were the reason for some of my troubles. I matured when I stopped blaming them completely for my misfortunes and the things that happened. I matured when I started to be accountable for my part and deal with myself. I knew I had to do major forgiving...because it had been done for me.

In my isolation, God dealt with me about forgiving the people who hurt me. Holding on to hurt was how I had gotten so far gone. Although what had been done to me was wrong, my response and reaction had been the real issue.

Bad things are inevitable and cannot be stopped. Our responses and reactions to them can be Godly in nature and show we are children of God. That's one part of accountability. It's being responsible for *your* response to a situation whether or not it's beyond the scope of your control. The second half of accountability is understanding and accepting that you may never get the apology you are owed. Vengeance belongs to God and retaliation should never be your response.

I had to learn that lashing out not only hurt people who did nothing to me, it hurt me, and the people who hurt me weren't much bothered at all. They went about their business. That's when it dawned on me. I had to really forgive because I was the one being held back, not the people who had hurt me.

I wholeheartedly began to forgive my ex who fathered my child for not being there when he should have been and for not helping me through that process, seeing as how I didn't get myself in that predicament. I forgave him so that spirit of rejection, bitterness and hurt could be uprooted in me and die, never to have a chokehold on me again.

I forgave Tee for feuding with me and not being as supportive as he had been in the past. I had to forgive him because it dawned on me he had no idea how unfamiliar and unplanned all of this change in me was. He was hurting me because he simply didn't understand. How could I be angry forever when he didn't know?

I had to forgive my college ex with whom I had countless verbal altercations and constant drama. I had to forgive him because rage and anger had a hold on and were manifested in me. That caused a sharp tongue to fester in me and I automatically went into self-defense mode over the slightest, silliest things.

I needed to forgive on a huge scale so I could be free to walk on the water of my life and approach Jesus with no obstruction to my faith that might cause me to sink.

I never got the apology from my child's father and he's still happily living his life. Had I not forgiven him I wouldn't be happily living mine. That's the key. You've got to forgive FOR YOU. Your life, your next level, your freedom depend on it. Until you've been forgiven and have forgiven as you need to, you won't really be free. Whom the Son sets free, and in turn, forgives others, is really free indeed.

I also had to truly, for real, for real forgive myself. I had to see myself the way God sees me and let things go. When I was able to do so, I began reattaching the pieces onto my crown to the point where they no longer were in danger of falling out and being lost. When I stood up, dusted myself off and forgave myself, that's when I reclaimed my place as a princess, no longer a prodigal.

So many times we hold on to what God has let go of. So many times we continuously find new ways to beat ourselves up or allow people to beat us up when God has patched us up and sent us on our way to live, forgiven, washed clean and free of the things we've done. That's what I did. I let what some people had to say and their opinions become a prison. It doesn't have to be that way. If God forgave you, then *you* need to forgive you, too.

One of the people I like in the Bible is David. I *like* him. David was a hot mess, but guess what David also was? Favored by God. Yep. He was a king and he was favored. I like to say he was flawed but favorited by God. (I know "favorited" isn't a word in the dictionary, but it's an Adara word so just flow with me. You're already over a hundred pages in with me so flow with me, please?)

David was favorited. The Bible depicts David as "a man after God's own heart" in 1 Samuel 13:14 and Acts 13:22. He was extra special to God. Well, if you read your Bible and study David, you'll see how over and over he did things that would not be extra special, let alone pleasing to God. I'm talking about criminal, perverted, deceptive, hot tempered, just "a hot mess" kinds of things. David was someone who peeped at a married woman bathing on the rooftop, then slept with her, got her pregnant and had her husband killed to cover up his sin. All of that drama existed way before TV shows like *Flavor of Love* or *Love and Hip Hop*. *Flavor of Love* was my show, I'm not even going to lie, but my point is the Bible is filled with drama and dramatic characters and goodness, was David one of them!

David was that guy who was ill-tempered, who not only would bust you up, but bust up your whole family, your neighbors, even your cows. He almost did it to Nabal, but he didn't because he had some sense spoken into him.

So anyways, like I was saying, David was not a model citizen if we go by human standards. But he was "it" to God. In spite of the horrible things he sometimes did, he still had the grace and favor of God on his life. He was favorited.

David was it, no matter what he did, because of his heart. God said so in 1 Samuel 16:7 NLT. He said, *"The Lord doesn't see things the way you see them. People judge by outward appearance, but the Lord looks at the heart."*

We would normally think of David as a no-good, low down, dirty criminal who belonged in prison for the things he did, and possibly we'd be right in feeling so except for two very simple words: BUT GOD!

I might belong in prison for things I've done and how careless and reckless I was…BUT GOD!

Isn't it dope and so cool how God loves us and forgives us no matter what dumb, crazy, rebellious stuff we do? He examines our hearts and makes His judgment. He extends us His love and grace and forgiveness when we have a heart for Him and that hungers for Him. He embraces us, forgives us and takes us back—no matter what. That's true love. That's what you do for your favorite. That's what was done for me, and that's what God wants and actually can do for you, but again...only if you want it and you let Him.

Can you think of a better deal than that?

Chapter 12

Walking the Christian Road

Less Traveled

One of the most common misconceptions about being a Christian, if not the most common amongst young Christians ages 18 to 35, is that being a Christian is boring. Oh, I have heard it, day in and day out and truthfully, I used to think so. I feared being a Christian, and if that's how you feel towards this lifestyle, that's what it is: fear.

It's a spirit, actually. Without being extra churchy and preaching a ten-point sermon to you, fear is a spirit sent straight from the enemy to keep you from having a real relationship with God, but you don't have to live under it or with it.

Fear is designed to make you move further and further away from something because you don't know what will happen or how you will handle it. Think about the person with a fear of heights. They have a fear of being too far from ground because they don't know what might happen when their footing is not secure on ground level. Think about the person scared of rollercoasters as well as heights. A person with those phobias or fears will not willfully hop on the tallest rollercoaster in an amusement park. A trusted friend usually has to reassure and comfort them to get them to even consider venturing onto the ride.

Anything that ignites or instills fear and worry is not of God. Because, as the Bible tells us in 2 Timothy 1:7, *"God has not given a spirit of fear, but of love, power and a sound mind."* I learned this Scripture as a child and have never forgotten it. It is a key Scripture to hold on to. When I learned this particular passage, it was for comfort after a bad dream, but I came to understand the meaning of this verse and to apply it for myself, especially throughout this process. God would never, ever cause us to worry or be afraid of anything, especially Him. We are to fear the Lord, as in honor and reverence Him, but we don't have to have a phobia or fear of Him. So, worrying or fear that choosing God will not be the right choice is sent strategically from the enemy.

The phobia or fear of living a godly lifestyle because it may be boring is designed to keep you from pursuing God. In fact, the exact opposite is true. Living for God has been the most fun I've ever had. I've had more fun doing what's right than I ever had trying to force myself to like the wrong things I was doing. Although living for God is the road less traveled, it also definitely is the road less tragic. I've come to see that doing things God's way is the best way, the safe way and it certainly can be the fun way.

I didn't always feel like this. I had preconceived ideas which fed into the myths about being a young Christian. I equated being saved with staying in my house, being cooped up all day long with my Bible and not doing anything, all to avoid sinning.

You can opt to live your life that way, but you definitely *will* be bored and frustrated. Moreover, you'll waste time that Jesus himself has given to you. Jesus said, "I have come that you might have life and have it more abundantly" in John 10:10. He never said, "I have come so you could have church service 24/7 or sit at home and never enjoy yourself." He said He came to give life.

God desires for us to enjoy our lives—even in our youth. Ecclesiastes 11:9 tells us to enjoy our youth, but remember we each will give an account to God for all we do. Reading and understanding this was critical for me because this Scripture challenged me to reevaluate the things I "enjoyed" and determine whether they were worth it in the long run.

I had to get my life in order so I could receive the life Jesus was talking about—life here and life eternally ever after. I began to receive it once I decided to walk this walk without faking it. It happened when I stopped trying dibble and dabble in a Godly lifestyle, taking only the parts of the Bible I liked and tossing the rest to the side because it challenged me.

When I stopped faking, that's when I got my real life, but it wasn't a simple one-two step. It wasn't a familiar electric slide. It was like joining a dance group or squad with no prior knowledge of dance. Getting my life in order required work, personal discipline and the desire to be a part of the team. I had to break everything down and start over. I had to figure out piece by piece, with God's help, what it meant for me to really do this thing called being a Believer. The change started from the inside and grew outward. I had to have an attitude and mind adjustment, then the behavior followed. I got tired of having one foot in and one foot out. I got tired of feeling bad and dirty after doing something I knew I had no business doing. I grew tired of my prescheduled, premeditated sin.

I made up in my mind and heart that enough was enough. When I made up in my mind I truly was going to set *and keep* my affections, emotions, focus and desires on God and things above, that's when change happened. I broke free of confusion when I decided to be all or nothing for God and that I wouldn't turn back. I was tired of being lukewarm and sometimey with God. I was determined to stop taking advantage of God's grace to fulfill my selfish desires with what made me feel good for a moment.

Once this new mindset set in and my heart was in agreement, it became easier to walk away from things that were not God-like. The desire and foul taste to go clubbing, drink, smoke and have a man make me feel good eventually faded away.

I began to converse with myself as I navigated through the purging process. I began to see things as very black and white. For me, everything became either yes or no. Either whatever I was doing or involved with would be pleasing to God and bring Him glory or it wouldn't. That's how I stopped going to clubs until the wee hours of the morning just so I wouldn't be bored at home. That wasn't bringing glory to God. It's how I stopped occasionally slipping up with my ex, stopped having sex with him after we broke up. That wasn't bringing glory to God and sex outside of marriage had grave costs, a few of which I'd already paid and couldn't afford to pay again.

I began to be "about this life" instead of just saying I was about it. It was what God wanted. He desires all or nothing. His Word says He would rather us be hot or be cold than lukewarm (Revelations 3:16). He is not sometimey or choosy with us, and He desires the same from us. There was bigger and better I could and should have been doing with my time, my talents and my energy.

So I started to. I channeled everything into working out my soul's salvation with fear and trembling (Philippians 2:12).

And it was all good...until the enemy used one of his age-old fear tactics, one that had been successful with me before: the fear not of being bored, but of being boring. It crept up in me and I had to wrestle with and overcome it.

For so long I cared too much about what people thought of me. That care became a prison. I determined to stay out of the prison of opinion. I knew I wasn't boring. I was the life of every party I attended. I was that friend who hyped everyone else up during pregame. I don't have a shy personality. Rather, I have a sense of humor and boldness, so I *knew* I wasn't boring. You can't ever let the enemy use the good qualities about you against you. God fashioned you the way you are for a reason: to be used for His glory.

I learned to arrest those negative thoughts about myself that were lies. I was not socially inept. I had a great personality and I got along with people. I prayed and battled against the spirit of rejection. I fought back against the enemy's attacks against my mind. I made choices to reject sin. I refused to be made out to be a monster or otherwise wrong for choosing to give up my old life, and I would encourage you, if you are in that place or that's your current situation, to do the same. You'll never be wrong for it. Choosing Jesus will never be wrong, not in this life or the next.

If you choose Him in this life, you become a candidate for the next life. I came to an understanding that liberated me, an understanding that gave me the strength to stop trying to rationalize and reason with anyone who didn't understand my choice to change my life. Jesus understood my choice and that became enough for me. That became the strength I needed to stand firm and not fall prey to what people had to say.

See, the problem was never that I was clubbing or hanging out every night. The problem was I did it for all the wrong reasons. I was immersed in a fast lifestyle of sex, partying, substances and loud, profane behavior. Nothing about that life was productive, Godly or helping me to grow as a woman. So, I walked away and chose the road less traveled.

As I mentioned earlier, I walked away from two people very close to me in my pursuit of God and being closer to Him, but they weren't the only ones. I had to stop hanging out with my party circle. I unfollowed many people and eventually deleted all my social media. I wanted no ties to anything or anyone that could potentially cause me to stumble or fall backwards while I was taking steps to get free. I made some abrupt choices when I decided I was all in. I went cold turkey and it was hard. I went through this withdrawal from the world because I wanted to be free. Many nights were spent alone in my apartment in prayer and in tears as I went through that purging.

Breaking an addiction through withdrawal takes a person through so many different changes and feelings. Everything not like God had to be spiritually regurgitated no matter how good or bad the taste or how much it hurt. That's what happened to me. I went from one extreme to the next. It wasn't easy to sever ties with the world and sever the soul ties I had with people, but it had to be done. I really wanted to be free. I allowed God to strip me of everything that was not like Him and make me over into a true disciple.

So, everything had to go.

Everything.

Walking the Christian road less traveled is not comfortable and it's not easy. My bad attitude and bitterness had to go. Harboring ill feelings when I said I had forgiven was no longer acceptable. As human beings, our nature is to gravitate toward what's comfortable and familiar, even if we know it's dangerous. There were times I backslid. I backslid and repented until I got sick of the back and forth and being in and out with God, until the taste and desire for things I once desired made me nauseous and ultimately were removed. This is what I did until I really settled in my mind that no matter what, I was going to do this, this living for God. It didn't come without a fight. It was, still is and always will be a fight against my fleshly, selfish old ways, a fight against temptation and a fight against the demonic forces that target young people specifically to lure them away from what's right and from what they've been taught. The good news is we can win that fight with Christ.

With Christ, I *am* winning that fight.

Deciding to be a Believer didn't come without a desire to slip back into the world. Some parts of me longed for the way things were before Christ; they had been that way for so long. I'm not ashamed to say this here or any place I share my truth because I've been freed.

In the beginning phases of my new walk and deliverance, I missed the way the old life felt when it felt good. I missed the floating feeling marijuana gave me and the way Hennessey made me feel relaxed. I had equated those things to fun, so when I gave them up, I felt like I was missing out. *That* was a lie. You aren't missing out on anything when you decide to chase after God and pursue righteousness. Never let anyone make you feel differently. You have the right to and you should walk away from anything and anybody who doesn't lead you closer to God, no matter how long you've spent together.

I can't stress enough that changing my life and choosing God really was a process. Most people recovering from addictions don't change on their first attempt. Recovery and breaking free from sin are no different. I didn't break free in one shot. I wish I could tell you I did, but I didn't. I had to embrace change. Change had to be adopted in every area of my life. Change had to start on the inside and grow outward—not just lay on the surface (remember the bamboo analogy). I began to talk like a person who loved God, to act like a person who loved God, to dress like a person who loved God. I began to honor God in all my ways, but this change didn't come without falling short and making mistakes.

As much as I would like to sound all perfect, like this walk and being a Christian are like floating on a cloud 24/7, they are not. Every day is not cake and flowers. It gets hard and comes with a cost, but the Godly life is very worth it.

I will never go back to the way I used to be before I accepted Jesus into my heart. Once you've made that choice, never go back. In my opinion, living my life sold out to Christ, having to let things and people go is a small price to pay and indeed a reasonable sacrifice when I look at what He did for me. Sacrifice, as I've said, is the nature of love. Since He sacrificed for me and gave His all, how can I not love Him and do the same?

It's human nature to want to be comfortable. We don't like to embrace change which challenges us or confronts us in the areas in which we need to be challenged and confronted. We like to hide behind our masks and pretend because that's the easy way out—the familiar route. We run. I ran, and eventually I fell into a ditch. That's what happens. You run from God and you run right into a ditch each and every time you run, so it's best to not run.

I knew walking the road less traveled would cost me close knit relationships and friends and even some family wouldn't understand. I had to choose between what society says and what the Word of God says. But if God knew my heart, why couldn't I just lay low? Why did I have to be on the front lines and give my all? The answer was simple: because Christ didn't have that attitude and He did not half step. Christ gave His all. Of course He had desires and ideas for what He would have liked to happen in His life, but ultimately He prayed for what God wanted. His final prayer in the garden of Gethsemane was nevertheless, not my will, but Your (God's) will be done. That has to be our lifetime prayer if we are truly walking this walk and being about this life, no matter how old or young we are. We have to want the will of God for our lives, no matter the cost or discomfort. Jesus did and we can too.

Christ is the best example we have of what it means to suffer and endure to the end. He's our greatest example of being a child of God. Jesus Christ encountered every single problem or plight we could possibly ever encounter and overcame them; the Bible tells us this. As long as we are in Him and He is in us, we have that same power to overcome.

This was so comforting to me to know. He knows how I am feeling and why I feel what I do. Jesus was faced with the same prospect of having to choose to serve God at a young age. He was twelve when the time came to make His choice to serve God. Even the people closest to Him—his own family—didn't quite get it. Still, He went about The Father's business. That was comforting and gave me strength when I started down this road.

I decided to stop straddling the fence because it was dangerous. One wrong slip or fall could have been fatal. If Jesus returned while I was engaged in any activity not Godly or Christ-like, I would not inherit nor enter heaven. Knowing that became enough for me. I began to see all of my choices through that lens and my view changed. I eventually stopped playing church. I stopped living a lie Monday through Saturday, then fronting like I was so saved on Sunday. Faking it was exhausting, time consuming and crippling, and not only did I know I was faking...others knew, too.

One of the final defining moments in deciding to stop running from and playing with God was getting noticed coming from a party in another state by someone who knew me though my parents' ministry. I was ashamed and embarrassed for myself, and I made my parents look bad. I was already speaking in ministry at this point—proclaiming the Gospel yet I was leading a double life. That felt dirty and I no longer wanted that feeling. I had access to much better than that low standard of living. Living out lies was no longer fun, so I stopped.

I dumped out a chest full of club clothes and bagged them up in black trash bags to be discarded and given away. I got rid of the bottles stocked under my kitchen sink for a rainy day or for when I was bored. I severed ties to my associates and peers who were party promoters, bartenders, go-go/exotic dancers and street pharmacists. I became intentional about guarding and protecting myself, with God's help, from dangers seen and unseen.

I will never go back. You couldn't pay me enough. I know I made the right choice, the smart choice and although everyone has not been pleased—people who knew the old me, even some of the "saints"—God is pleased and that's what matters.

Being a prodigal princess and finding my way back home wasn't just about coming back in the literal sense. It wasn't just about stopping ungodly behavior. It was about my heart. My heart had to find its way home. I had to get back to the place I knew as a child wherein I longed for the things of God. Children are so pure and innocent. They desire God and they have a pure connection to Him. I had to get back to being that little girl who enjoyed church and the things of God, that little girl who held revivals on the playgrounds and baptized her dolls. I had to get back to that place, and I did. My prodigal heart came home.

You have the right to choose the Lord for yourself no matter what anyone else thinks about it, no matter how many times you've failed at it. You have the right and are allowed to choose God. When you do, the good news is He takes you back.

My encouragement and advice to you would be to not let anyone or anything stand in the way of you getting your identity and finding peace, purpose, forgiveness and love in God. The Bible poses a profound question to us in Romans 8: 35-39. It says, "*Who can separate us from the love of God?*" then proceeds to provide the answer. Nothing. This question is applicable to you and I. Who and what can keep us from God? Nothing and nobody physically can, therefore nothing and nobody should be able to keep you from finding and experiencing the love of God for yourself—not friends nor peers nor family nor even other believers.

Oh yes, this is the part where I open up about how not everybody reppin' Jesus Christ or saying "I love God" will be thrilled about *you* living for Him. There are several reasons for this, including but not limited to their own insecurities, jealousy, double life and just being down right full of themselves. Remember, there's nothing new under the sun. This happened before, at least twice in the Bible. This type of hate occurred when Jesus went to hang out with Zacchaeus in Luke 19 and it's also found in Luke 15 when the prodigal son found his way home.

Remember, when the prodigal son came home, although his father was overjoyed, not everyone else was. His brother, his own flesh and blood, was not happy. His older brother was so hung up on the fact his younger brother had strayed and now was being celebrated. He was bent out of shape because he felt entitled to recognition and reward for staying, not straying. He was focused on the wrong things, and he criticized his father for celebrating his brother's return. That's exactly what happens when "saints" forget that but for the grace of God, they would be "ain'ts".

The funny thing about the prodigal son story—and my story, too—is that the people who should have been happy about a lost soul finding the right way were not. Instead of being happy I found my way back, people chattered and talked. People critiqued my going into ministry. I won't lie like it wasn't so hurtful and discouraging to me at first, but I didn't let it stop me. I knew what I was called to do and I was going to do it. I had come too far to let the opinions of people oppress me any longer. Sad sight to see if you ask me, but that's how it happened. The good news is this did not stop the prodigal son, it didn't stop me, and it does not have to stop you. Not everyone will be happy and celebrate your decision to choose God, to walk in purpose, have peace and live for Him. That is okay because the person who will ultimately care, the person who matters, will be pleased. God will be pleased.

Walking this road less traveled so that you can enter into His rest in paradise matters more than what anyone says or thinks about you. Now, I walk this walk proudly with my head held high. I'm living boldly. New challenges and battles arise, but I stay strapped. I'm surviving. I'm floating, not sinking or drowning. This portion of my life is about gaining resistance and gaining new strength now that I've gotten past those old struggles, strength to walk the road less traveled with boldness and confidence.

Perhaps this is you and you need help finding the strength to stick with your new life in Christ. Here is a prayer you can pray:

Lord Jesus, I come to You asking You for strength to live for You. I desire to be all or nothing for You as You gave your all and stopped at nothing for me. Lord I ask you for boldness and confidence to stand on the Word and lean on You. I thank You for unconditionally loving me and for choosing me. I pray for courage and a heart to always choose You no matter what anyone else chooses. I ask for the confidence to choose Your will always and a made up mind to live for You always.

In your name I pray,

Amen.

Chapter 13

When Walking the Road Less Traveled, Walk it Well

I wish I could say my current walk with the Lord is 100% perfect, that I never stumble or fall anymore. I wish I could tell you I never cry or feel like giving up. I wish I could tell you I never wonder if this life will be all worth it—if Romans 8:18 really is true, if my suffering and what I deal with now really doesn't compare to what will come in this lifetime or on the other side.

I wish.

But I can't.

This walk is still work. It's going to be work for as long as you are alive. You have to keep pushing and keep moving. Your life, as well as someone else's, literally rests on that. It's do or die.

I've come to understand this for myself in the last twelve months because so much has happened that has changed my life, and I'm grateful for it all—the high, the low, the good, the bad and the ugly. Because all those things *have* worked out for my good. That's what the Bible tells me and reminds me in Romans 8:28. That Scripture is why I try not to worry about anything or get worked up. It all is a part of the plan.

God's plan.

Still, don't think it's that simple. I have to push myself every day to believe those things. I have to speak the Word over myself and train my mind to believe it. I've begun to train my mind to see the good and the GOD in everything, even when it does not look good and doesn't feel good. There are days when I want to give up, shut down my ministry and sink into the back of my chair. Then, there are days the emails and messages pour in— about how my ministry has changed someone's life—and I can no longer make this about me.

Of all the messages of encouragement and thanks I receive daily, there has been one I have not been able to shake. It was from an international follower (from Chile, I want to say) who messaged me to tell me my account literally helped her bounce back from depression and suicide.

2016 marks year two in ministry for me. I am not full time yet, but I know it will come to that eventually. For the last two years, I've been preaching, ministering and serving while maintaining a full time job. At one point, I had two jobs and I also am pursuing my master's degree in education. I'm doing a lot on every side of my life, secular and sacred. It really is God who keeps me because I wear a lot of hats at once, and if I didn't know or have the Lord, I would go crazy, especially with regards to the ministry side. I say this frequently, and I'll say it again. Nobody with a sound mind just decides to go into real ministry because of everything that comes with it, like having to lead by example, carrying other people's issues like your own, always being on the front as an example and all the work that is required in order to have a thriving, effective, successful ministry in the Kingdom. A synonym for ministry, if you ask me, should be work, or tests of faith which I will elaborate more on in this last and final chapter.

This is the chapter in which I open up to you about current Adara. Present day Adara. Minister Adara.

The princess restored now faces a different kind of struggle, but she bears it with pride and honor. I'm talking about ministry. This is my now, but I must give a disclaimer, the same disclaimer I gave in the very beginning. The things in this chapter may shock you and arrest your attention, but I am okay. I repeat. In spite of what you read in the remainder of these pages, I am in my right mind, I'm alive and I am good because God is so good and He is a keeper.

So, about this ministry stuff...let me tell you everything I've experienced thus far. I'm going to recap the things that have happened with me as a result of saying yes to God.

Ministry, in my opinion, is like marriage. It is a lifetime of work. Once you accept the call and say I do, what you do no longer becomes about you. It now is about serving someone other than yourself. It's about being a part of something greater than yourself and sacrificing for that something greater. The day you say you will, you immediately come second. You will come second until the day you enter into eternal rest. There will always be someone to minister to. That's why you can't just jump into this thing called ministry of your own doing, without being Spirit-led and called.

This thing called ministry will affect your entire life and at times will test you *and* your faith.

Let me break it down for you so you can understand.

I've learned I can't pour from an empty jug and I can't help someone else if I haven't covered my bases or taken care of myself. Ministry can take a toll. No matter in what capacity you serve in God's house, you are part of the ministry. No matter if you vacuum the carpet or preach in the pulpit, you need to take care of yourself and be a good steward over your life. Knowing yourself and how you operate and work best is of the utmost importance. Knowing what (or who) works against you is equally as important. The Bible tells us God's people perish, or fail, for lack of knowledge. Tired soldiers aren't as effective in battle against the opponent.

Oh, and yes you have an opponent.

Trust and believe, once you switch sides to be on God's side, you now have a clear opponent, the devil who can't stand you for choosing God. From the day you decide to be a prodigal no more and you make your way home, he wants nothing more than to try to stop you from following through with your choice to serve God. Don't worry so much about him, though because he's not really that special. I know how to beat him and since you bought my book and read it this far without tossing it, I'll be sure to share how to do it, to tell you how I'm beating him.

When I got serious about God and said I would serve, it wasn't about being seen. Whatever needed to be done, I did. If it meant preaching, cool. If it meant greeting at the door, cool. I was just glad to be found and to be home. I learned true repentance is coupled with the willingness to do the lowest, least important job. Besides every job in the Kingdom being important to God, being willing to do what others might not was the least I could do for what He had done for me. That is the essence of ministry.

The prodigal son had a similar humbling experience. When he came to his senses and repented, he said to himself, "I am no longer worthy of being served in my father's house; I deserve to be a servant." He vowed to humble himself and serve and do whatever his father asked. That's how it was for me. When I realized just how far gone I had been before I found my way and the Lord reeled me back in, I realized I had no right to be all about self anymore. I had no right to try to elevate myself. My place was at the feet of Jesus, ready and willing to serve.

That's what being the prodigal princess meant to me. I turned around and went back to my father's house and also to my Father's house—to church where I humbled myself and got involved. I didn't do it for the attention or to make anyone happy. I did it because it was the least I could do compared to what had been done for me.

This planted the seeds for my small portion of ministry to grow. Whereas the wrong seed once grew in my life, once I humbled my heart and took on the mindset and attitude of a servant, then the ministry God placed in me was able to be birthed.

It has been an interesting journey. Every day is different. I am living out my purpose and would never trade any portion of it. It's a blessing. This ministry has brought me fulfillment I never imagined because I now do things the Godly way.

Remember the opponent I mentioned? The moment you say yes to serving God in any capacity, you have an opponent. The enemy. He was there before, but now he's worse than ever. Oh yes, he couldn't stand you while you were in the world and darkness, but as soon as you see and accept the light, he really, really, really can't stand you. He begins to expedite the contract he has out on you, to steal, kill, and destroy your life, your dreams, your freedom, your peace, your hope, your joy and your faith.

The enemy is the ever so Level 5000, annoying adversary and opponent known as Satan. He's a very real enemy who does not play fair. Actually, we shouldn't play with him at all. In the past two years, and especially this year, I've seen just what lengths he will go to try to stop us from being who we are supposed to be and from doing what we are called to do.

I've dealt with attacks against my health before, but in the latter portion of 2015, the enemy upped the ante and let me know that from here on out, we would have to duke it out and fight. It became very real to me he was willing to do anything and everything to stop my mission, to stop me from progressing forward and to intimidate me into giving up on ministry and even my faith. Once I climbed to a new level, out from his place of hiding came a new, more cunning devil. I got a very real wakeup call and reality check—confirmation that ministry and everything that comes with it would be my life.

This confirmation of the call on my life came the morning of Tuesday, November 10, 2015. The thief wasn't able to reach me or steal from me in the ways that had worked in the past. I no longer needed to drink and drown my sorrows. I was past the need to flaunt my body for attention. I was past the hunger for marriage. So he had to find a new way to get at me. I will never be a Christian who gives more credit to the enemy than he is due, but I won't front...he is very cunning and clever to strike when I least expect it. Level 5000 clever.

This day, I was on a spiritual high and he caught me off guard.

The night before the 10th had been a regular night. I had a full day at my job, I posted quotes and memes and I was going about my business. I never saw anything life-threatening coming at me. In fact, I was still on a cloud from the Sunday before. That Sunday, I had received a fresh outpouring of the Holy Spirit, like I never had before. The next night, Monday night, I was still floating. It felt like it had only been mere hours. Well, because we have a very, very petty enemy who hates to see us with joy and strength—hence, why he tries to steal it away—I was about to be up for the fight of my life...literally.

The morning of Tuesday, November 10, 2015, I woke up from my sleep around 2 or 3 a.m. and realized my phone was off the charger. I looked at the time and put my phone back on its charger. Usually I sleep on the left side of my queen-sized bed because it's closer to my nightstand and light, but for whatever reason, this morning I fell back asleep on the right side of the bed.

The next time I woke up, it was somewhere between 5 and 5:15 a.m. and I awoke to a man in my bed. I thought maybe I was having an erotic dream of some sort, but that was not the case. I reached out in the dark only to touch the arm I thought I saw— and it was real.

There was an uninvited man in my bed with me.

I sleep very freely in the comfort of my home, so at this time, I was only in my undergarments. When I looked down, he was in his too. He began to massage my face and my breasts, and I knew what was about to happen. My heart sank. You see this type of thing in Lifetime movies, but you never expect it to happen to you.

I snapped out of the daze of my sleep and I started to scream. I screamed and pleaded and begged for him not to do what I anticipated was his objective. I asked what he wanted and begged him to leave. I promised I wouldn't tell and I would be quiet if he would just leave. That didn't work. Before I knew it, he was halfway on top of me, and I was on the verge of a sexual assault, rape, or worse.

This was real. I had two options. I was either going to fight back and fight this man off or let this happen to me and possibly die right there in my bedroom.

I gathered all of my strength and although half-naked, terrified, humiliated and angry, I went into war mode. I fought back. I pushed and pushed and wrestled, and we fought to the floor.

The door was cracked because he hadn't closed it all the way behind him when he came in. We both eyeballed it. He got off of me and moved toward the door to close and lock it. If he were able to do that, I was sure his intention was to follow through with what he came for.

I WASN'T HAVING THAT.

My survival, out for blood, "get you before you get me" instincts kicked in. I rushed him as I called out the only name I know when in times of trouble. I called on the name of Jesus. I screamed the blood of Jesus! I screamed, "No! No! No! You will not do this to me. The blood of Jesus!"

My New York, slightly hood side came out and I fought. I two-pieced him while screaming "the Blood." Before he had a chance to lock the door, I rushed him and forced all of my weight on him so he fell back on to the door, pushing it open.

We were now in my hallway directly across from my bathroom where I knew I could be heard. We stared each other down for maybe two seconds. As he moved toward me, I again started to scream and work my amateur boxing moves. I continued to yell, "Get out of here! Get away from me. The Blood!"

The more I yelled the words "the Blood," the more aggressive and agitated he became. I knew that the name of Jesus still had power and that at the sound of it, demons tremble and get aggravated. I was staring down a demon. It was bigger than the man trying to assault me. As the Bible says in Ephesians 6:12, we never fight against people, but against principalities, wicked forces and rulers of the darkness of this world. I was two-piecing one of them.

In the midst of our fight, I looked at his face and what I saw confirmed he was possessed. His eyes were bloodshot and had anger in them. He also had a dark, dark aura exuding off of him.

I fought. I screamed and continued to scream, "The blood of Jesus!" And just like he did to Jesus when he tried to tempt him, the enemy spoke back to me. Through my intruder, the demon sneered at me. As we wrestled and he forced me to the floor, he said, "Who is your god? Where is he? WHO IS YOUR GOD?" He kept shouting and I kept screaming.

I'm here today because I fought with all my weapons and didn't let what I saw or felt fake me out. I was determined to live and not die.

To live and *not* die.

The walls of my apartment were thin. Praise be to God, after what seemed like forever, someone from upstairs heard my screams and cry for help. Two people came to my aid, breaking us up and apprehending the guy.

I started to cry. I was traumatized. There were multiple people in my apartment, I was half-naked and exposed, and I was on the floor weak from having just fought off a grown man.

This attack rocked my world. It woke me up from my natural and spiritual state of slumber. I just had been introduced to another level of spiritual warfare. As believers, we know all things are spiritual first. While I never negate the fact that I was humanly attacked by a man, I am clear it was at the release of my opponent. I give God the praise, however, because I survived to tell others.

If you are going to be about this ministry life, you had better be ready. It comes with a cost, whether it's having to deal with people who don't feel like you are qualified to preach, not being able to enjoy simple luxuries like vacations whenever you want, or maybe increased spiritual warfare like what I was up against. To whom much is given, much is tested and required. This was my test and this experience was required of me.

At the time of my attack, I was engaged in a new level of warfare. My role in ministry had shifted, and I had just received a fresh wind of the Holy Spirit. The attack was the backlash. This experience was required to teach me that my first response should always be to pray. Just like the Bible says, men—and that implies women—are to always pray and not faint. When our enemy comes against us, our first response should be go to God.

He should never be our last resort. This experience heightened my senses to the need for unceasing prayer.

The second thing I learned from this was to expect backlash whenever you get major breakthrough. Sure enough, the last few times I have preached or ministered, during or directly after each instance, some sort of backlash or attack has come. Now, I expect it and prepare for it because the kind of funny thing about the enemy is that if you pay attention, he's kind of predictable. That's why it's important to keep your eyes, both spiritual and natural, open at all times. The moment you close your eyes, you have the potential for collision or harm. The moment you stop paying attention and close your spiritual eyes, you become vulnerable to spiritual collision and attack. The awesome thing is I've peeped his game and I now know how it goes.

As far as my intruder, I didn't press charges against him because I knew him. I later learned he was off his medication when he attacked me. He wandered over to my apartment and broke in. I didn't press charges, however I made it known he needed professional help, and he got it. My apartment was secured, I got beefed-up security around my place and I even got a couple of wonderful surprise gifts just in case any other demon wants to try me in that way again.

The biggest reason this had to happen to me was to serve as a reminder that no matter what, I am equipped to fight the good fight of faith and live for God. Truly, nothing and no one can separate me from the love of God...not even the petty workings of the enemy.

In the days after the attack, the trauma and the fear of retaliation or a second attack haunted me. My faith was shaken and I became a prisoner in my home. For a while, I tiptoed around the place I paid my hard-earned dollars for and acted like I was caged or in jail. I showered with the doors locked and not a minute longer than I had to...with a knife close by. I was unable to be in my undergarments too long without being covered, and every night, I triple-checked my windows and doors. I frequently woke up in the night after bad dreams in which I relived what had occurred. It was hard to regain control and not feel violated.

It took much healing, prayer and support for me to bounce back, but I did. Through the prayers of the people closest to me, support from my parents, talking to a professional psychologist/life coach and increased security around my home, I was able to recover. I was able to shake this experience and not let it consume or haunt me because I kept pushing and ministering.

This is the first I've ever openly talked about the attack. The very thing the enemy tried to silence actually doubled up and came back stronger as a result. I kept doing what he tried to intimidate me from doing—serving and ministering—and the more I did it, the stronger I got and more control I regained. Every now and then a weird feeling may arise, but I don't shrivel up in fear or hide out in my house afraid to leave. Jesus came so we could live abundantly. Living in fear is not included in His description of abundant life, so I refuse to make it a part of mine. Thanks be unto to God who gives us the victory, today, I am healed from this.

This attack, still vivid in my mind, also serves as a reminder that I have a mouth to open and speak and call out for help as well as two holy hands I can lay and two faithful feet I can stomp. Using my God-given weapons saved my life that day. My prayers, not letting fear grip me and actually fighting back saved my life. I encourage you all to always be strapped with your weapons— which are the full armor of God, the safety found only in the power in the Blood of Jesus and hands that can two-piece somebody, if need be. Even though I'm not a fighter because I'm saved, and we bless God for that, my hands still work. Just saying.

Through this experience I learned to always be ready. Spiritual warfare is very, very real. The higher you go and harder you go in God, the harder the enemy will "for serious" go at you. But it's okay...because we win. We've already won. The cross won. The blood Jesus shed on the cross already defeated the enemy so it's all good. Still, that doesn't mean we can slack or sleep, have our heads in the sand or be oblivious to that sneaky, conniving enemy who is waiting for just the right opportunity to catch us slipping.

And catching us slipping doesn't necessarily equate to luring us into committing sin or falling short. On the contrary, sometimes it's simply us not watching out for him and forgetting that he strikes when we least expect it. Hence the term "like a thief in the night" which because the night is when we let our guard down as we sleep and rest.

I got my wake-up call because, even though I was in ministry, I had been asleep. I was not aware how close to me the opposition was. I didn't fathom it was literally on the other side of my bedroom door. You and I cannot be asleep. There's a prowler lurking and searching for the chance to *try* to hurt us or stop us. (Notice how I emphasize the word "try." That's the most he can do.)

As servants in the Kingdom called to purpose, soul-winning, deliverance and healing, we cannot be asleep. We cannot be asleep as Believers as a whole. I was asleep and then I woke up. It wasn't like I woke up from a wonderful dream. I woke up from what I thought was a nightmare, but was very real. I experienced firsthand what happens when you decide to be sold out to God, be about this ministry life and try to bring others along with you. Before you decide you want to go into ministry or be on the front lines, be advised the front lines come with a cost. I knew that, ran from it, accepted it, then got a good dose of it in a way I will never, ever forget.

Ultimately, I share that experience to let it be known we never stop facing difficulty as Believers, but we are on the best team and serve the best God. I share this experience to let someone know being a Christian comes with challenges, but we truly overcome by the blood of the Lamb and the words of our testimony. Even in writing the pages of this book, I've been ministered to and gotten stronger and been healed from the tiny remnants of the hard things about my life. This is what it means to be overcome by the words of your testimony. The more you share what God has done for you, the stronger you become. That's why I wrote this book.

I've overcome many things in my short twenty-five years of life that should have and would have killed me, but didn't. My life was spared because of God's grace. I found my way back home to God, and although every day is not perfect and at times it is even hard, I am way better off now than where I was without God in my life.

This prodigal princess has been redeemed and restored and she now rests because God rests within her. God is with me and I will not fail. If you are like me in any shape or form or you can relate to anything written in this book, as long as God is with you, no matter what is thrown your way, no matter what obstacles you face, you will not fail either.

If God could take me back, a princess who lost her way and became a prodigal, then remake me into a princess again, good as new...

If God could do a major clean up on aisle 5000 to bring me to this current committed, sold-out place...

Then, He can "for serious," for real, for real, do that and more for you.

Love, *Adara*

Afterword

Well, that's pretty much it. I told you this book would be a good read, and not just because I wrote it. (Well, okay, maybe just a teeny bit because I wrote it.)

Just kidding.

It is my sincere prayer this book has blessed you in some way. I pray wherever you are in your walk with Christ, you find some comfort in knowing there are other Christians out there who have gone through some things and survived. Whatever you are going through, you too can survive.

If you are a person who read this book because you were intrigued about this Jesus I go so hard for, it's my prayer you see why I love Him and why I go so hard. Hopefully my story's moved you to want the same.

As I've said many times, in the simplest of descriptions and job titles, I am an encourager. I encourage people to try Jesus. I encourage people to live for Him and I encourage people to never give up on doing so. Yeah, yeah, I preach the Gospel and I love it and I'll be doing it until the day I cross over into eternity, but the first and foremost job I have is that of encourager and hype man. I'm the hype man who gets the crowd pumped for the main attraction of the event or show or party except now, Jesus is that main attraction. He restored this princess so I can now be a small part of His big show.

Part of my job as the hype man is to make it live and poppin' enough for the main attraction to be on the scene. That's what I do. All day. Every day.

I'm a prodigal princess, just a former wild and wayward girl turned down and turned all the way around into a for real preacher and hype man—well, hype woman—for the real, true artist, Jesus Christ.

Thank you for reading my truth.

Yours truly, with Christ's love,

Adara Butler

About the Author

Adara is a minister and Christian inspirational speaker born, raised, and currently living in New York. She enjoys traveling, meeting new people, and spending time with her family and friends. She is currently enrolled in school pursuing her first Master's degree in Adolescent Education with a concentration in History. *A Prodigal Princess* is her debut book.

Visit the author's website at **www.adarraaa.com**
Visit the author's social media:
Instagram: @ adarraaa
Twitter: @ adarraaa
Periscope TV: @ adarraaa
Facebook: Adara Butler

Made in the USA
Middletown, DE
14 August 2016